POPULAR
POTTERY

By the same author:
Teaching Today: Pottery (Batsford, 1981)

POPULAR POTTERY

Shirley Bates

B T Batsford Ltd, London

To Ralph, Julia and Terry

First published 1982
© Shirley Bates 1982

ISBN 0 7134 4168 2

Printed in Great Britain by Butler & Tanner Ltd, Frome, Somerset
for the publishers
B T Batsford Ltd, 4 Fitzhardinge Street, London, W1H 0AH

Contents

Introduction

Today, pottery is perhaps one of the most popular of all hobbies and interest in the subject is ever-increasing. The greatest problem for those wanting to take up pottery as a hobby for the first time and to experience the many delights of working with clay is to find a pottery class with a vacancy. All over the country evening and part-time pottery classes are over-subscribed and there are long waiting lists for vacancies, for so often these vacancies tend to be 'dead men's shoes' — in other words, people rarely leave a class because of boredom; it is nearly always a case of *having* to because of a domestic move or similar problem.

I have always been delighted by the regular attendance of my pottery evening class students — nothing short of the impossible will keep them away.

Young mothers find working with clay particularly relaxing after a harrowing day with a young baby or young children. As a follow-up, of course, they get enormous pleasures from teaching their own children as they grow up to work and play with clay and proudly bring the 'first pots' along to the class to be fired.

At the other end of the life-scale are the retired people who wish to take up a hobby that will provide fulfilment, happily use up spare time and even provide a small income or, at least, cover its own costs.

Lastly, of course, pottery appeals to the busy business man, as working with clay will enable him to find relaxation from the many tensions he experiences in his everyday work. In this case pottery tends to have a therapeutic effect, as it not only provides mental and physical involvement in a way that is totally removed from the daily stresses but also provides people with the opportunity to mix with others from different walks of life who share a common interest and love of working with clay.

Unfortunately occasions arise in most family lives when responsibilities at home make evening out very difficult to arrange, and it is at times like this that assistance is required to help set up a small pottery workshop at home. This is not nearly as difficult or as expensive as it may sound — instead, pottery at home can become quite a lucrative hobby, providing amusement, company and pocket money.

It is with these aspects in mind that this book has been written. It is hoped that it will provide assistance to *all* hobby potters, whether they have the good fortune to be able to attend a class which provides the facilities of a pottery studio, kilns and teacher, or whether they are in a situation where they must work at home without these advantages.

With this book I shall aim not only to provide a self-tutor and friend for the hobby potter but also to give a wealth of ideas and useful tips for the potter who has already had some experience with the magic of clay-work. It is intended that this book should be used in a similar fashion to that in which a favourite cookery book is used. In the middle section of the book various types of pottery will be described and illustrated and recipes provided for the making, decorating and firing of individual pots.

During the many years I have spent as a pottery teacher and lecturer I have bought numerous books on pottery, but have always found it a problem to suggest *one* book for the hobby potter which will give sufficient information and ideas, in simple terms, about how 'to do and to make' pottery. This, then, I hope will be *the* book!

Colour Plates

1. Wrap jug and a coiled vase showing incised patterns — tenmoku stoneware glaze

2. Two press moulded dishes decorated with coloured slips and 'feathered'. Transparent earthenware glaze

3. Slabbed jigsaw pots — stoneware glaze with resist decoration

4. Large slabbed sculptural pot — stoneware

5. Flower-shaped pot made using coils and slabs — stoneware

6. CHAOS — slabbed letters made from red and grey clays, unglazed

7. Owls — pinch pots — note textures

8. Collage of eight tiles depicting African dancers — stoneware

9. Three thrown bowls

10. Triple thrown pot — stoneware

Acknowledgements

To my evening class students who inspired me and caused me to write this book. To Paul Bolton, Jean Gilson and Martin Brierley who assisted me with the photography. To Michael Whittlesea for his advice and assistance with the line drawings, and to Simon Tuite for his guidance and encouragement.

1 About Clay

What is clay and where does it come from? In simple terms, the clay we use to make pots is dug from the ground, washed to remove foreign bodies, sometimes mixed with other types of clay, and bagged in polythene ready for our use.

It is a fascinating material, and as there is plenty around it is inexpensive and easily obtainable. Most people find it easy to handle and experience great excitement when using it to fulfil their creative instincts. With clay one can experience a tremendous amount of emotional satisfaction and, indeed, frustration when things go wrong! It has a variety of qualities that no other raw material has, and with water added to it can be used over and over again — until it has been fired in a kiln.

It is the firing of clay in a kiln that provides a pot with permanency, for once clay is heated to around 600°C (1112°F) it changes it state and becomes 'pottery'. Pottery cannot ever be totally destroyed. Once a pot has been fired it can be broken up into small pieces, buried deep in the ground and lost, but remember that many thousands of years hence someone could come along and put together all those pieces and there will be your pot again! A serious and rather mind-bending thought when making pottery — the message behind it is: don't fire a pot unless you are satisfied

Etruscan pot

with it and want it to be kept. Clay can always be reused, but pottery is there for posterity!

Most people, given a lump of clay, can sit down and make quite an attractive piece of pottery — this ability is in us from our childhood when we revelled in the 'mud pie' era. The problems that arise are usually in the creation of the permanent pot, and this is where a few simple lessons need to be learned and an understanding of the material acquired. The shrinkage of clay needs to be understood and recognized; it is quite different from plasticine, in that as it dries it shrinks and becomes more fragile, and when it is fired it shrinks yet again. Although clay has little value when dug from the ground it has tremendous potential, since with only a little imagination and knowledge beautiful and expensive looking objects can be made.

The purpose of this book is to explain and simplify the problems that beset the hobby potter and to contribute to the delights of working with clay.

TYPES OF CLAY

When studying a pottery catalogue it can often be very confusing to see the large variety of clays listed — of course they all have their individual purposes, but for the hobby potter and for general use I would suggest that initially clays should be considered under the following headings:

Red terra-cotta clay: This fires to an earthenware temperature of up to 1080°C (1976°F).

Grey general-purpose clay: This fires to a stoneware temperature of up to 1260°C (2300°F).

Grogged grey or 'toasted' stoneware clay: This is suitable for coiling, slab-work and throwing (e.g. St Thomas's Body) and which fires up to a temperature of 1260°C (2300°F).

Crank-type modelling clay or marl: This containing a lot of coarse grog, is for modelling and sculptural purposes only, which fires to temperatures up to 1260°C (2300°F).

Local clay: Should there be deposits of local clay that can be dug, it must be prepared before use. This can form a very interesting experiment, and the following advice may well be of assistance if such a project is attempted:

1 Having dug the clay or removed it from a river bank, break it into small pieces and remove any foreign objects such as stones or leaves. Ideally the clay should then be left to weather for a year or more, but this is not usually practical, so the following more rapid processes have to be used.

2 Cover lumps of clay with water, having first placed them in a bin. Leave for a few days, stirring from time to time.

3 Brush the clay and water slurry through the coarsest sieve you can get (a garden sieve is good to start with) in order to remove more of the rubbish. Add more water as necessary and sieve through progressively small-guage sieves once the larger lumps have been reduced.

4 When the slurry is smooth, scoop off any excess water and spread the clay to dry on a large plaster slab. (A slab can easily be made by mixing

potters' plaster or fine builders' plaster with water and setting it in a large plastic bowl or tray.) Turn the clay from time to time as it dries.

5 Wedge and knead the clay when suitably plastic and store in polythene or airtight containers or bins.

6 It is advisable to do a firing test on the clay before spending much time making objects with it. To do this, fire a tile of clay to biscuit temperature 960°C (1760°F) and check shrinkage and warpage. Sometimes these faults can be corrected by the addition of a proprietary clay.

Most clays dug locally are fun but are rarely suitable for general use. Experiment only will show what your clay is best suited for.

PREPARATION

All clay must be wedged and kneaded before use (see illustrations). This really is important and must not be ignored — there are no short cuts!

Wedging: Take a large piece of clay, knock it into a block shape and cut it in half with a length of cutting wire or coarse fishing line. Throw one half down on to the other with as much force as possible. Repeat this process a number of times, for it is this action that forces out the air pockets. Inspect the clay for air pockets each time you cut it.

Kneading: There are several methods of kneading, but I prefer the 'ram's head' method. This is done by taking a lump of wedged clay that you can comfortably handle with two hands and forcing the hands down, with maximum pressure being exerted from the wrists. Lift the clay at the end farthest away from you and push forward onto it (the shape will resemble a ram's head, hence the name). Repeat the process several times and your clay will be kneaded. It is the same technique as the baker uses with his dough. N.B. If the clay is too soft it will firm up if kneaded on a plaster bat or on a wooden table top. However, should the clay be of the correct consistency to start with, it is best to wedge and knead it on a stone or slate bench, as this will not absorb moisture from the clay. If the clay is too hard, cut it into pieces, sprinkle it with water, wrap it up in polythene and leave it for a few hours before wedging and kneading.

Demonstrating the 'Rams head' method of kneading clay

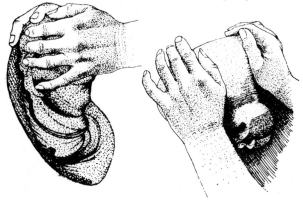

ABOUT CLAY

DRYING

Because of shrinkage it is imperative that finished pots are dried evenly, so when drying green ware (i.e. unfired pottery) do bear in mind the following points:

a A large pot or a pot of uneven thickness needs very slow drying.
b Always avoid uneven drying such as placing a pot in a draught or allowing one side to be heated by sunlight or a radiator.
c Dry tiles slowly between bats and sheets of dampened newspaper.
d Take especial care when drying pots with handles or spouts. Remember uneven shrinkage will cause warpage or cracking.

It is helpful to understand the stages that clay passes through as it dries. These are:

Liquid or slip state: This is the wettest. Slip is used for decoration, casting, and joining clay.

The plastic state: This is the usual condition for making pottery, by throwing, coiling, slabbing, modelling etc.

The leather-hard or cheese-hard state: At this stage pottery can be turned on a wheel, and handles and spouts are fixed. Slip decoration and burnishing may also be done at this state.

The dry state: The clay is now hard and brittle and is lighter in colour. Brush decoration is often done at this stage, using metal oxides and stains. All pottery *must* be in this condition before firing. Unless it has been burnished it will usually have a dusty surface and not feel really cold to the touch.

STORAGE AND RECYCLING

Storage: Clay should preferably be stored in lidded bins. Supplier usually pack clay in polythene which keeps it in good condition for a long time, provided the polythene is not punctured or torn. However, it is not practical to use the clay from the wrapper — it is far better to place it in a small dustbin or a bin with an airtight lid. If the airtightness is suspect, place a sheet of polythene under the lid. If more than one type of clay is stored try to keep them separate by polythene wrappers in the bin, or in separate bins. It useful always to have a bin or container for used unfired clay which can then be recycled for future use.

Recycling: Into the 'Used Clay' container place all unfired clay that is too dry for ordinary use (if in large lumps break up with a mallet first). Reject pots that are not good enough to fire will always recycle, as will lump clay that has gone hard due to exposure. The only type of clay that must *never* be put back into the recycling bin is that which is contaminated with foreign bodies, such as plaster. This must always be *thrown away*, as it will cause the clay to explode during firing, or pieces of the finished pot will chip and flake off after firing. When sufficient clay has been collected in the used bin, cover it with water and leave for a couple of days, stirring it occasionally. (This is a similar process to that used when preparing your own locally dug clay.) Remove excess water and then spread it onto fairly thick plaster or wooden bats to dry. It can then be returned to a bin in preparation for wedging and kneading. In this way very little wastage occurs. *Tired clay*: Clay can sometimes become 'tired' — just as we do! The reason for this is that it has been in constant use, and the symptoms are that it will suddenly collapse, splitting as it folds. This is because the clay has been overworked, and the cure is to leave it to rest unused for a week or so and then to mix it with some new clay before wedging and kneading it ready for use.

GROG

This is a finely ground pre-fired clay which, if added to a smooth clay by kneading it in, will reduce shrinkage and add strength whilst making pots. It will coarsen the surface texture but is ideal for slab pottery, model making and, in moderation, adding to clay to be used for the throwing of large pots. By adding grog to clay the need for the hollowing out of models is not so crucial, provided the drying process is observed; this is particularly useful when working with young children. As an alternative to grog, ordinary sand which has been seived may be added to clay — this will have a similar strengthening effect.

AIR-DRYING CLAYS

I feel mention should be made in this chapter of the new air-drying modelling clays that are now available from several pottery material suppliers. These are quite expensive to buy, but for people who do not possess a kiln or the facility to use or make one, the world of working with clay is opened up instead of being a process and craft which has to be denied. Objects made with this type of clay harden when exposed to the air. It is not a rapid process, so there is plenty of time for work to be carried out, and drying can be retarded by covering the work with polythene. Left uncovered, the finished work will become fully hard in two or three days. It can be decorated after half a day and when completely dry can be burnished or polished. A gloss finish and protection against moisture can be achieved by the application of a cold glaze which is usually supplied with the kit. All spare pieces of the clay can be reconstituted, even when hard, if so desired. Pottery made with this type of clay can be hardened in an ordinary domestic oven, but if, on the other hand, a kiln becomes available at a later date, then the pots can be fired and glazed in exactly the same way as with ordinary clays.

Kneading clay by the spiral method

2 Setting up a Pottery Workshop

Many people have the urge to set up a small pottery working area of their own at home, either in a spare room, in a shed or even at the end of a garage, but are usually nervous of what this entails and the cost involved.

In this chapter I shall make suggestions regarding the setting up of such an area and the acquisition of simple tools and equipment, and mention the techniques of building simple kilns. I shall also include information on the firing of kilns and recommend simple safety precautions.

It is, of course, ideal to have a work area that can be kept exclusively for clay work, but this is not always possible, and a shared work area is quite feasible provided there is a shelf where drying pots and pots in the making may be stored safely. A small cupboard is a useful addition and, if lined with polythene, makes an ideal damp-cupboard for storing unfinished pots or those requiring slow drying. Ideally, if you are to acquire a small kiln and produce a continual quantity of pottery, an area the size of a small shed 2 metres x 1.5 metres (6ft x 4ft. 6in.) would be most suitable, and I have included at the end of this chapter a simple layout plan, with explanations.

TOOLS

As with all crafts, each craftsman needs his or her own tool kit, and this can be very inexpensively obtained. Of course, if you have a little spare money or are offered a present of some pottery tools, these can be obtained from most pottery suppliers. However, first of all I shall concentrate on the home-acquired variety and then I shall list some very useful extras that can be purchased from suppliers that I shall mention at the end of this book.

Modelling tools: These can be shaped very easily from wooden lollipop sticks.

Cutting wire: For cutting clay from a large lump or for cutting free a pot from a wheelhead after throwing, use a piece of fairly coarse fishing line or fine wire about 30 cm. (12 in.) long and attach a button or a piece of wood at each end as 'handles'. I find brightly coloured buttons best as the wire is then easily found and easy to hang up.

Spike: A sharp metal knitting needle or a darning needle in a cork (a sharp bradawl will also do), for cutting shapes in rolled-out clay or for trimming pots on the wheel.

A rolling pin — if not available, trim the end off a broom handle.

Hessian (or an old sack cut up) for rolling clay out on. A piece of linen

14

Useful tools and equipment

could also be used for this purpose. It prevents the clay from sticking to the work-top.

Sponges: A fine one for smoothing damp clay and a larger coarse one for cleaning up.

Sandpaper (or a kitchen scourer — the green material variety): for smoothing off dry clay.

Slats: For rolling clay out to even thickness (e.g. 30 cm. (12 in.) long x 5 mm. (¼ in. thick). These can be varied in thickness according to requirements.

Old cutlery: knives, forks and spoons in any condition have many purposes.

Paintbrushes: Collect various sizes of the thin variety for painting on oxides and stains when decorating.

Polythene bags and ties: Bread bags are very useful if saved for this purpose. Part-made pots may be kept moist in them until you are ready to continue the making process.

Incised buttons: Useful for making attractive press-in decorations on flat clay or around the sides of round pots.

Cylindrical card centres: Collect them from toilet rolls, carpet rolls, etc. Tins are also useful and, when used with a piece of newspaper to prevent the clay sticking, assist in the making of wrap pots.

Scales: These are useful for weighing out materials and clay and can often be obtained very cheaply from jumble sales.

Containers: Collect a variety of containers such as bowls, jugs, buckets, an old cup sieve (for making hairy clay!), jars with screwtop lids and, of course, a dustbin or two in which to store clay.

Overall: the jacket variety is most useful, and a man's old shirt is perhaps the most useful and cheapest (worn back to front).

SETTING UP A POTTERY WORKSHOP

EQUIPMENT

Certain tools and equipment must at some time be purchased from a pottery supplier, and I list below some of the basic items:

a Two sieves (or lawns), one 80 mesh and one 120 mesh. These are used for preparing glazes and slips.

b A lawn brush — used in conjunction with the sieves.

c 12 cm. (4½ in.) funnel.

d Tile cutters of various shapes, square, round, hexagonal, etc.

e Slip trailers — or small detergent bottles can be useful if saved for this purpose.

f Metal kidneys for smoothing clay.

g Rubber kidneys for smoothing clay.

h Harp (for cutting and thicknessing clay) and spare wires.

i Turning tools.

j Boxwood modelling tools.

k Wire-ended tools.

l Lightweight aluminium whirler, for decorating pots and making coil pottery.

m Plaster moulds, for making matching sets of dishes, mugs, bowls, etc.

n Kiln — a muffle (inside) measurement of (30 or 45 cubic cm. one or one and a half cubic feet) is best to start with.

o Kiln furniture — i.e. props and bats (shelves).

MATERIALS

a Clay — grey, firing to stoneware temperatures
        — red (terra cotta) firing to earthenware temperatures.

b Plaster of Paris — potters' plaster

c Transparent glaze — firing to an earthenware temperature of 1080°C (1976°F).

d Opaque White glaze — firing to an earthenware temperature of 1080°C (1976°F).

e Oatmeal or tenmoku glazes — firing to a stoneware temperature of 1260°C (2300°F).

f Bentonite (a suspender that prevents the glaze, when mixed, sticking to the bottom of the bucket!)

g China clay and ball clay for mixing slips.

h Bat wash and silica sand — for protecting kiln shelves.

i Oxides and stains such as manganese dioxide, red iron oxide, copper carbonate, blue stain and yellow stain.

j Cones 04, 07, 8 (Orton variety) for telling the temperature of a kiln if you do not possess a pyrometer.

KILNS

Generally potters who wish to work at home and produce a regular supply of pottery, or those who wish to experiment with the wonders of clay and glaze, save up and buy a small electric kiln — say about 30 cubic cm. (one

Packing a small kiln (electric)   *Unpacking a large kiln (electric)*

cubic foot) muffle size (that is, the inside dimension). A new kiln will cost around £200.00 (in 1981) and a second-hand kiln — if you are lucky enough to obtain one — about £50.00. Personally, I find the Hymus Essex kilns the best value for money and the simplest to operate and repair. (I give the name and address of the supplier at the back of this book.)

Home-made kilns: The two most popular — particularly for groups of home potters — are sawdust kilns (usually made from an old dustbin) or clamp kilns, which are made by digging a hole in the ground. I give below details for building each of these.

The clamp kiln: Dig a small pit in the ground (putting aside the turf) measuring about 60 mm. (2 ft.) across and 25-30 cm. (10-12 in.) deep. Position three pieces of metal tubing approx. 30-35cm. (12-14 in.) long in triangular formation in the pit. Next, place some pieces of dry wood and some paper in the bottom of the pit and light it. When it is burning well, gently pile on some sawdust, which will deaden the flames. Smoke should now be seen to be coming from the ventilation tubes, showing that the sawdust is smouldering. Embed the pots in the sawdust and cover them with more sawdust. Replace the turf over the mould and then place an old dustbin lid over the clamp in case it should rain. Leave the venting tubes

17

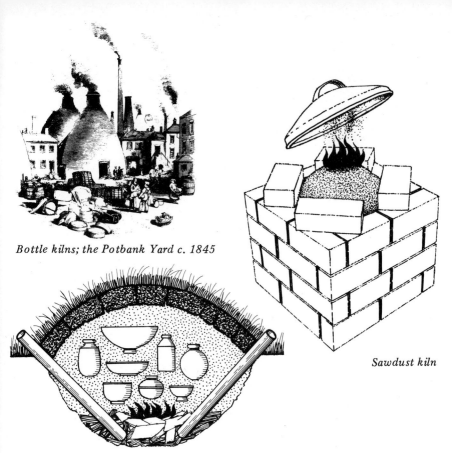

Bottle kilns; the Potbank Yard c. 1845

Sawdust kiln

Clamp kiln

open to the air. Smoke should issue from the tubes which are not facing the wind. When the fire has burned out — this usually takes between 12-16 hours — rake the pots out; you will be fascinated by the results.

The sawdust kiln: There are several ways of making a sawdust kiln. Two of the most common methods are:

a   A metal bin (e.g. a small dustbin) with a few holes punched in the sides for ventilation and a lid on top.

b   A cubic shaped brick-built kiln, using ordinary housebricks. Small gaps should be left between the bricks for ventilation and an old dustbin lid (metal variety) placed on top.

In both cases layer sawdust in the kiln, embedding the pots about 5-8 cm (2-3 in.) apart. Start the sawdust burning from the top by lighting a twisted piece of newspaper and placing the dustbin lid on top, slightly propped up for ventilation. When the sawdust has finally smouldered away the firing is complete. This is likely to take between 16-24 hours — the longer the better. ALWAYS allow kilns to cool completely before removing lid and unpacking — this will prevent unnecessary cracking.

Tips: With all types of sawdust firing it is a good experiment to burnish the pots (preferably using terra-cotta clay) with the back of a metal spoon

18

handle, using a circular motion. This should be done at the leather-hard stage. When really shiny allow them to dry completely before firing. The fired pots will have a lovely dark shine finish, with no glazing necessary. Should there be any local clay available, dig it, make pots and fire them in this way — the results can be quite fascinating and it is fun to be 'master' of the whole process, from digging to firing.

Electric Kilns

Care and servicing:
If you possess an electric kiln it should give you many years of faithful service provided a few basic rules are followed, so before discussing the use of a kiln, i.e. the packing and firing, I shall look in more detail at the care, simple service and adjustments that concern a kiln and its aids.

Bats (or shelves): Ensure that you have the correct sized bats. They should allow at least a 2.5 cm. (1 in.) gap all round when placed inside the kiln. For example, if the muffle size of the kiln is 30 cm. square (12 in. x 12 in.) then the size of the bat should be no larger than 25 cm. square (10 in x 10 in.). It is of the utmost importance to leave this gap in order to allow the hot air to circulate inside the kiln — otherwise the elements will quickly burn out. When new, bats should be coated with a bat wash (a combination of alumina and china clay or zircon and china clay) mixed to a thin paste with water. It is also advisable to sprinkle silica sand onto the bats as well, for the bat wash and silica sand together will protect the bats and help prevent pots sticking to them should the glaze run at high temperature.

Bungs: Never push the firebrick bungs tightly into the vent or spy-holes of a kiln. As the kiln heats up the bungs will expand and consequently be difficult to remove when cold, and possibly break. When inserting the bung, push it in and then withdraw it a fraction — this technique will usually solve the problem.

Props: These are the spacking tubes that separate the shelves inside the kiln. Generally it is advisable to purchase the plain tubes as these do not chip and become damaged as easily as the castellated variety.

Cracks: If cracks appear in the kiln and are fine ones, leave well alone as they are usually only expansion cracks. Should larger cracks appear it is advisable to wet the crack and then fill it with a fire cement such as 'Pyruma'. Slowly fire the kiln to around 400°C (752°F). when dry, to set the cement.

Elements: To extend the life of the elements in a kiln it is advisable to vary the temperature of firings as much as is possible — e.g. after a stoneware firing, follow with a biscuit firing rather than repeat another stoneware firing. Do not touch the elements unless absolutely necessary, as they become very brittle. Keep them clean by dusting away particles of dust and pottery with a soft brush.

N.B. NEVER push mothballs into kilns in order to create a reducing atmosphere — the effects on your pottery might be interesting but your elements will be ruined!

Pyrometer

Pyrometers: If you already have a pyrometer and suspect its accuracy it may well need to be sent back to the manufacturers or serviced by a specialist.

Firing a Kiln
New Kilns

As these will not have been used before they must be 'broken in'. To do this, switch to 'low' or about one-third of the full temperature with no pottery inside the kiln and ventilation bungs out. Leave the kiln on for about 4 or 5 hours. This will have a gentle drying-out effect on the fire-bricks and cement, which may still contain moisture from the time when the kiln was built. It will help the elements, of course, if you take the kiln up to around 1100°C (2012°F) whilst still empty in order to give them the protective coating as described earlier in this chapter. When this has been done your kiln is ready for use.

Packing a Biscuit

a   Ensure that the pottery to be fired is absolutely DRY — a rough guide is that it should not feel really cold to the touch, and if a finger is rubbed over the surface then a fine powder should be deposited onto it.

b   The pieces of pottery will not stick together in the kiln as there will be no glaze on them, so pack them inside and on top of one another. However, take care not to wedge them tightly together, and leave gaps at the sides and at the top of the kiln as the pots will expand slightly before they start to shrink. Shrinkage at this stage is around one-eighth. Place the larger and stronger pots at the bottom of the kiln and let them support the lighter ones. If really delicate pottery is to be fired, use bats for support and separation.

c   Commence the firing, with bungs out, slowly.

Packing a Glaze Firing

a   Check that any surplus glaze has been sponged off from the bottom of the pottery and from the sides up to about a quarter of an inch from

20

the bottom if the pottery is to be fired to stoneware temperature. Remember that any deposits of glaze will melt in the heat and cause the pottery to stick to the bats. Sprinkle the floor and bats with silica sand as this will help to prevent any overglazed ware sticking.

b Pack the kiln with pieces of pottery so that they do not touch one another. If you push one pot up to another until it just touches and then withdraw it a fraction you will know it is not touching. Also it is wise to place pieces of similar height on the same shelf – this will economize on space. Arrange shelves and half shelves in such a way that the kiln will hold as much as possible. A full kiln will always produce a better firing than a half-empty one. Remember to leave enough room for cones if they are to be used. It is important that the props supporting the shelves should be placed directly above one another – use three props in a triangle in smaller kilns and five in larger kilns.

c Fire the kiln in the same way as for the biscuit firing, the only difference being that it will take longer for the kiln to reach the glaze fired temperature the next day, particularly if it is a 1260/80°C (2300/36°F) stoneware firing.

Firing schedule

The safest and easiest method of firing a kiln is to adopt the schedule mentioned above. ALWAYS place a notice above the kiln describing the type of firing and there will be little chance of things going wrong. If you happen to be out or held up when the kiln reaches its maturing temperature another member of the family or a friend can be asked to turn it off for you. It is also useful to keep a firing log or chart as firing times are usually similar unless there is voltage reduction or surge. A typical example of firings might be:

Overfired kiln showing damage to kiln and to pottery inside – it has melted into a solid mass

21

Kiln on low	Kiln up high	Kiln turned off
Sat. 4 p.m. Bung out	Sun. 9 a.m. Bung in	11.35 a.m. (960°C) (1760°F)
Sat. 4 p.m. Bung out	Sun. 9 a.m. Bung in	12.50 p.m. (1080°C)(1976°F)
Sat. 4 p.m. Bung out	Sun 9 a.m. Bung in	2.45 p.m. (1260°C) (2300°F)

Measuring temperatures There are several methods for measuring the temperature inside a kiln. The most common of those used nowadays are pyrometers and pyrometric cones. A pyrometer is a clock-type temperature indicator, usually calibrated 0°C − 1400°C (32°F − 2552°F) on an edge-wise mirror scale.

Pyrometric cones differ inasmuch as they determine the satisfactory completion of a firing. Their compostion and structure is such that they bend when subjected to heat for a period of time − i.e. their operation is dependent on 'heat/work' and not temperature − though the end result is virtually the same, as the pottery is satisfactorily fired either way. Cones are graded according to the amount of heat work they can withstand and are placed inside the kiln in alignment with the spy-hole. There are many types of pottery, fired at many different temperatures, but in general I would suggest that one should use the following temperatures as a guide:

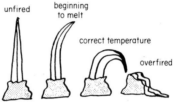

Melting stages of a pyrometric cone

Type of firing	Temperature	Orton cone	Nearest staff. cone
Biscuit	960/980°C (1760°/1796°F)	07	06
Earthenware Glaze	1060/1080°C (1940°/1976°)	04	02
Stoneware Glaze	1260/1280°C (2300°/2336°F)	9	9

SAFETY IN POTTERY AREAS

In industry today the safety precautions imposed are infinite, but for the home potter I would recommend that the following simple rules are followed:

a Wear an overall when working.

b Wash your hands thoroughly before eating and do not eat or smoke when working.

c Ensure there is adequate ventilation in your working area.

d If firing a kiln, have some sort of timer to remind you that it is on so that you do not forget it and so overfire your pottery and perhaps also burn out the kiln and its elements. A heat fuse installed at the time of purchase is a good way of preventing this happening and costs very little compared with the repair of a damaged kiln. A heat fuse may alternatively be added to a kiln at a later date as an extra, usually by the manufacturer.

e Do not allow children into the kiln area when a kiln is being fired, and do not allow them to touch the chocks in the door or on the top of the kiln.

f Do not open the kiln until it is quite cold.

g When mixing glazes wear some sort of mask — the nurses' disposable masks are best and cheapest (Kleenex variety, obtainable from a large chemists).

h Place a sign in an obvious place in the house indicating that the kiln is being fired and at what temperature it is due to mature and be turned off.

i Obtain a CO_2 fire extinguisher and affix it to a wall near the kiln so that it is easily accessible — just in case!

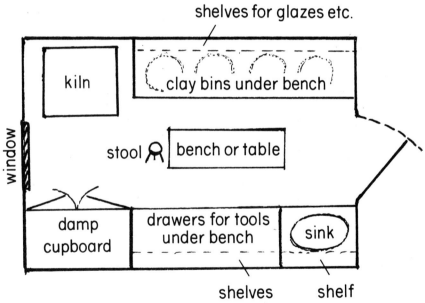

Pottery shed (scale approx. 1 : 30)

3 The Pinch Pot

In this and the following five chapters I shall provide the reader with a simple form of recipe book — the intention being to provide the hobby potter with ideas to assist the development of various clay techniques. However, in this book only the simplest combinations and suggestions will be made.

To begin with I shall explore some of the many techniques of pottery making without a wheel, and then I shall look briefly at simple pots that the beginner can make using a wheel. After giving a few recipes I shall make suggestions as to how clay may be used, on particular themes, by young children. These ideas are provided particularly with the mother with young children in mind, as a great deal of pleasure can be obtained by parents wishing to work with clay if the children can be occupied at the same time using the same materials and making simple pottery. It is a pastime that can easily become a total family pleasure and occupy many happy hours. In Chapter 12 I shall explain in greater detail how pottery can be made to pay for itself or even make a profit!

The pinch pot or thumb pot, as many people call it, involves the simplest and most satisfying activity of all. No tools are required for the process of forming the pot and it is, therefore, probably the easiest and best introduction to hand-building. It gives the beginner the opportunity of acquiring a feeling for clay. The action involved is a quiet one, requiring only a slow rhythmic action with the two hands, which is very therapeutic — usually one feels an enormous sense of calm whilst pinching the clay into the shape of a pot.

It is important to remember that whilst your fingers are pinching the clay the warmth from your hands will tend to dry it out, so it is best to start with fairly moist clay — the action of pinching will then harden and strengthen the pot as it is being made. Red clay is usually found to be best for this technique, as it is the most plastic. If a grogged clay is to be used it is often best to keep moistening the fingers during rotation — however, beware of using too much water, as it can turn clay into mud!

METHOD
Take a ball of clay a little larger than a golf ball, hold it in your left hand (if you are right-handed) and gently push your right thumb into the centre of the ball, leaving a thickness of about 10 mm. ($\frac{3}{8}$in.) at the base.

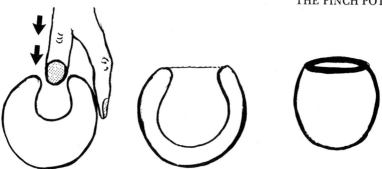

The action of making a thumb (pinch) pot

To make the walls, gently squeeze the clay between your thumb on the inside and your fingers on the outside of the ball. Rotate gently as you squeeze, trying to keep an even pressure as you work. It is important that the walls and the base should be of the same thickness before the pot is allowed to dry. Keep the rim a little thicker at the beginning — this will help to keep the pot in shape as it is being worked. However, each potter will find his own skills with practice. Do not despair if the first two or three pots do not succeed — co-ordination takes time to develop, as does the understanding of the handling of different clays.

There are many variations of the pinch pot. Having made your 'cup-shaped' pot there are many follow-up variations, some of which are mentioned below.

RECIPES AND IDEAS

Fruit or Nut Bowl This is quite simply made by adding a foot. This is done by rolling out a coil of clay and forming it into a circle. Lay the circular coil on the base of the pinch pot and pinch it out from the base. If the clay is slightly dry the coil should be joined to the pot with a little slip so that it is attached firmly to the pot. All kinds of interesting bowls may be made in this manner; small ones make ideal egg cups. Do ensure that the pot stands firmly on its foot — a rocking pot is of little use!

The Egg Join two pinch pots of the same size together, scuffing both edges first and joining with slip before smoothing over the outer surfaces. Roll the 'egg' gently on the table top to perfect the egg shape. When this has been done, and before you allow it to dry out, pierce a small hole through

Painting on slip before joining thumb (pinch) pots

Pinched bowl with foot added

A pig made by using two pinch pots

the wall of the egg in order to allow the air to escape. Handle very carefully after this has been done, as it is now very easy to squash or flatten the egg shape. If a hole is not made, the air inside the egg will expand during firing and cause the egg to explode — rather like a balloon bursting. These eggs can be made in various sizes and make lovely decorations, paper-weights and even door-stops if one end is flattened. Decorate by etching patterns into the clay or by using various glazes. The burnishing method, which I shall explain below, is also very effective.

Pebbles These are made in the same way as the eggs but patterned and shaped to imitate a real pebble. It is most interesting to try and copy an ordinary pebble picked up out of the garden.

Pomanders These are balls filled with scented herbs such as lavender or dried flowers and hung in wardrobes to make clothes smell sweetly. They are made in the same way as the egg, but holes are pierced in the sides to allow the fragrance to escape, two holes in the top to hang the pomander from and a larger hole in the bottom — large enough to fit a small cork — through which the pomander may be filled with the herbs.

Puff fish These are great fun to make — particularly large ones. Make the egg-shaped pot, add flattened coils to one end to make the tail and score on a fin-type pattern with a wooden tool or broken lollipop stick. Similarly add smaller flattened coils for the fins. Cut a fairly large hole with a needle at the other end to make the mouth opening and finish off by adding a round coil. The eyes may be indented or added by using small

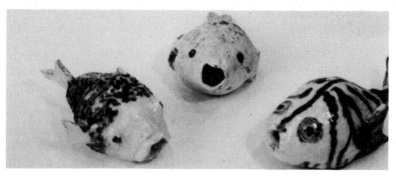

Puff fish

coils of clay stuck onto the main body of the fish with slip. Scale-like patterns may then be made on the body of the fish or patterns painted on with oxides before biscuit firing. If the fish gets a bit flattened during making, place a piece of paper over the mouth of the fish, pierce a hole in it and blow the fish up — like a balloon!

Bird ocarinas These are clay birds that can be played musically like a simple flute or pipe. The bird is fashioned in a similar way to that of the fish, but instead of cutting out the mouth, squeeze that end to make a bird's head (a third thumb pot can be added to make this shape if it is found to be easier). When the bird has been shaped satisfactorily, take a lollipop stick and gently push it through the bird's tail and in a straight line down through its belly. Then make three or four holes in a straight line down the bird's back to form the flute finger holes. These musical birds or ocarinas, as they are correctly called, really do play and are quite exciting to experiment with, musically and decoratively.

Flowers Very attractive and very delicate flower shapes may be made by placing three or four pinch pots of varying sizes one inside the other and pinching out the rims very finely. These rims, which form the edges of the petals, may then be tipped lightly with oxides and glazed in a simple glaze such as a white opaque. A few small pieces of broken coloured glass placed in the centre after glazing and before glaze firing can be very effective indeed. (See Chapter 9 on decoration for further details regarding this technique.)

Pinched flower decorated with iron oxide and an oatmeal stoneware glaze

Cartoon characters glazed with white opaque glaze and painted over with oxides before glaze firing

Cartoon characters These are enjoyable to make — particularly with and for children. Make an egg-shaped pinch pot and add to this a third pinch pot using slip and scuffing the surfaces to be joined. This will form the head. (Do not pierce any holes at this stage, as you will require the shape to be firm in order to work on it. Do this later). Add small coils of clay for the arms, scarf etc. and make a fourth pinch pot flattened outwards to make a hat — make a small coil to add for the hat band or ribbon. There are many variations on this theme and each potter will find his own favourite character. Decorate in bright colours. Often the best way to obtain these bright colours is to paint the oxides and stains on top of a white opaque glaze before glaze firing. However, be careful not to damage the powdery glazed surface whilst doing this. (See Ch. 9.)

Wind bells Make several pinch pots and shape them like bells. Pierce a hole at the top of the bell (i.e., the bottom of the bowl) before the pot dries and make a few clappers with holes in them by pressing small balls of clay between your thumb and forefinger to make small flattened discs about the size of a halfpenny. These bells are most effective if made in different sizes and the outsides textured with various things such as pieces of tree bark or buttons. Fire them once only to an earthenware glaze temperature of 1080°C (1976°F). They do not need to be glazed and this higher biscuit temperature will cause them to ring nicely. If made from a terra-cotta red clay they look very well if polished up with brown boot polish — this gives them a 'wooden' effect. When the bells have been fired, string the bells and hang them at different levels from a wooden or ceramic plate. Of course, don't forget to string the clappers inside the bells. If these wind bells are placed outside or in a draught they create a most attractive sound as they swing around.

Note: If made of red clay, fired in a home-made sawdust kiln and burnished they will usually turn out a beautiful black ebony colour after they have been polished with a wax polish.

Small plant holder This is designed to hold several small plants, bulbs, cactus or herbs and is made quite simply from a collection of pinch pots. For example, make seven pinch pots, join two of them base to base to form the centre pot and stand, and around this centre piece place five more pinch pots, joining them to the centre stand with coils which are smoothed to make a neat join. This type of multi-pot may be decorated in a variety of ways and looks very well textured, or made in unglazed red clay. The insides of the pots should be glazed to make them water-proof — a honey glaze is ideal for this purpose.

Crested bird This is just an example of the many ornamental pots that can be made using the pinch-pot technique. The crested bird is great fun to make and is made simply by combining pinch pots rim to rim and base to base. For the bird illustrated seven pinch pots are needed — two for the body, one for the stand, one for the tail, one for the head, one for the crest and one cut in half for each wing. Texture some parts and leave other parts smooth. Experiment and see what variations you can come up with. Note: Do not forget to pierce a hole in the main body of the bird before it dries hard.

Ideas for children Children are usually very good at making hollow pebbles and flat-bottomed egg cups (using one pinch pot). A 'bird's nest' can be made by scuffing the outside of a pinch pot with a twig or broken stick and filling it with small eggs — these can usually be made in a solid form if they do not exceed 20 mm. x 10 mm. (1 in. x ½ in.) in size (if they are made small they are unlikely to explode during firing). Another very good idea for young children, based on this theme, is the tortoise or turtle. It can easily be made from one pinch pot and a coil of clay that has been cut

Cat   *Crested bird*

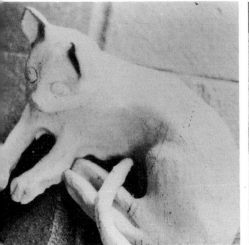

up into five sections — one for each leg and one for its head, on to which two little clay pellets are added for its eyes. Give the child a small stick and let him draw a shell pattern on to the backside of the pinch pot, thus creating the shell of the tortoise. Press the legs and the head firmly on to the shell, using the slip and scuffing method. Older children usually enjoy making cartoon characters, but they need to have had some experience with clay before attempting these more advanced techniques.

Further ideas using the pinch pot as the basic technique:

a Hedgehogs — two pinch pots joined to make an 'egg' — the face squeezed into shape, the spines made by pushing soft clay through a coarse metal sieve and applied to the roughened surface of the 'egg' with slip.

b Mice — make various sizes using two pinch pots, as for the hedgehog, and add a leather thong tail after firing.

c Fruits — all types of fruits can be made using this method — apples, plums, oranges, lemons, pears etc. The natural skin texture of the real fruits should be studied carefully and copied. This can be an interesting study. These pottery fruits placed in a fruit bowl look very effective and make a very good table decoration. They can also be made into condiment sets if a filler hole is provided at the bottom and pouring holes at the top.

d Vases — pretty spherical vases can be made by just adding a coil for the neck and teasing it out finely.

e Easter chicks — Make an egg in two halves and on the upper half add a piece of clay and fashion it into the shape of a chicken's head and also add a tail. Roughen the outside of the bottom half to make it look like a nest, make some little eggs to place inside it, sit the chicken on top and you have your Easter chick sitting on its nest!

Follow up After making pots, *always* allow them to dry slowly — in a damp cupboard if you have one, or cover them initially with polythene. If decorating with oxides or stains, do this any time *before* biscuit firing. It is usually best for beginners to use earthenware glazes, as the earthenware temperature of 1080°C (1976°F) that they are fired at does not usually cause distortion if the pots are slightly uneven. Alternatively, as I have mentioned above, make the pots with a red terra-cotta clay and burnish them at the leather-hard stage, then fire just once to 1080°C (1976°F) — but remember that unless you glaze the insides of the pots they will be porous.

4 Slab Ware

Slab ware — or pottery made from clay rolled flat — covers an incredibly wide variety of pottery. Many different items may be made using this technique, from simple tiles to the most elaborate lamp bases and vases. Before describing some of the many ways of approaching slab work, I feel I must emphasize right at the beginning two *very* important rules:

a the clay should be really well wedged and kneaded to ensure that all air bubbles are removed.

b slab work must *always* be allowed to dry very, very slowly. This helps to prevent distortion and the joins and seams are less likely to break apart. Wherever possible, the slabs should all be of the same thickness. If a slightly grogged clay is used and the slabs are allowed to dry slightly before building the pots, the whole building technique becomes very much easier.

METHODS

There are two basic ways of making clay slabs:

1 *Using a 'harp'*: Take a large piece of clay (preferably of a grogged variety) and knock it roughly into a cubic shape. Then take a harp and place it on the far side of the lump of clay with the arms of the harp upright. Pull the harp cutter towards you through the clay. In this way a slice of clay is cut from the lump of clay. As many more slices as are required may also be cut from the lump. By notching grooves up the arms of the harp and adjusting the wire, different thicknesses may be cut. Piano wire is best for this use. Harps may be purchased from pottery suppliers, or they can easily be made by bending a piece of metal rod or tube to form a three sides of a rectangle and stretching a piece of wire across the fourth side. The distance from the point where the wire is fixed to the ends of the metal rod should be the same at both ends — about 5 mm. (¼ in.).

2 *Rolling-pin techniques*: Due to its plasticity, clay may be rolled out like pastry using a rolling pin. First acquire a piece of linen-type cloth or

Rolling out clay

hessian (about the size of a tea-towel) and two sticks approximately 40 cm. long x 5 mm. thick and 3 cm. wide (16 in. x ¼ in. 1 in.) Place the lump of wedged and kneaded clay on to the cloth between the two sticks and roll it out, lifting it from time to time from the cloth. The sticks will act as thickness guides and the clay, when rolled out, will be an even 5 mm. (¼ in.) thickness.

Tips

a If your clay is rather dry, dampen the cloth slightly. As the clay is rolled out over it the clay will soften and become more easy to handle.

b When rolling out, don't try to push the clay *through* the cloth with the rolling pin! Remember you are trying to stretch the clay *over* the the surface of the cloth, in a similar manner as one does pastry over a floured surface. Push from *behind* the clay, don't lean *on* it.

c When lifting the clay from the cloth, try reversing the procedure – lift the clay and cloth together, turn the clay slab face down on to the left hand and pull the cloth away from the back of the clay with the right hand – it is always easier to pull cloth from clay than to try and lift clay from cloth.

RECIPES AND IDEAS

Tiles: Tiles are the simplest form of slab pottery, and can easily be made to any size or shape. If many tiles of a uniform size and shape are required it is advisable to purchase one of the large variety of tile cutters sold by pottery suppliers or, alternatively and much more cheaply, to make a card or board template to the size and shape of the tile required. To make tiles, first roll out the clay to the required thickness and either cut out the shapes with the tile cutter or place the template on the clay and cut around it with a needle. Remove the clay tile and, before placing it on a board to dry, score three or four grooves in the back of the tile (about 2 mm. ($\frac{1}{10}$ in.) deep). These grooves have a twofold purpose: they help to contain the adhesive if the tiles are to be affixed to a wall or board, and also they assist in the flat drying of the tiles and prevent the corners and edges curling up during this stage. Whenever possible, allow the tiles to dry very slowly between two sheets of damp newspaper placed between two boards. The drying process should take at least a week for the tiles to be absolutely flat.

Fish tile

TOP: *Wrap jug and a coiled vase showing incised patterns*

MIDDLE: *Two press moulded dishes decorated with coloured slips and 'feathered'*

BOTTOM: *Flower-shaped pot made using coils and slabs*

Slabbed jigsaw pots

Large slabbed sculptural pot

CHAOS — slabbed letters made from red and grey clays

Open-work tiles

Door plates

There are many many uses for tiles and they can be decorated in a variety of ways — textured, painted with oxides and stains, inscribed with a sharp tool, decorated with slips or with thin slabs added to make raised patterns. Alternatively, pieces may be cut out of them to give a lacework effect. There are many other possibilities, and I am sure each potter will discover his own. Some useful ideas for tiles are: tea-pot stands, table tops and trays, wall decorations, door names, house names and numbers, chess sets and draught boards.

The Anniversay Tile: this was a particularly nice idea that one of my evening class students designed; it certainly gave a lot of pleasure to the recipients. This was a tile shaped like a bell and was for a 50th wedding anniversary. It had the initials of the 'happy couple' inscribed on it and the date of their wedding. A small hole was pierced in the top so that it could be hung on a wall (see illustration). Similar tiles inscribed with the recipients' zodiac birth signs also make good presents, particularly if you can copy the old designs which are very artistic. These can easily be traced on to a piece of paper from a book and then transferred with a needle on to the smooth surface of the clay tile. Tiles depicting Christmas and Easter scenes are also very effective and give a lot of scope for inventiveness.

Zodiac sign — pisces

Anniversary tile

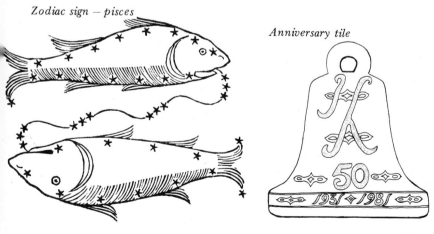

Ideas for children: Children will enjoy making tile jig-saws from quite a young age. Allow them to roll out, at random, a piece of clay (keeping it as even in thickness as possible) and paint a simple picture on it, using stains or scoring the picture with a pointed wooden tool. Then cut out fairly large jig-saw shapes, allow these to dry, fire them and stick them on to a board to form a picture, or just keep the pieces as toys. Alternatively make a collage such as an underwater scene with flat pieces in the shapes of fish, starfish, boats (half sunk), treasure chests, shells etc. Fire the shapes when they are dry and then make up the picture on a board that has been textured with polyfilla, paint the whole with powder paints and coat all over with a varnish.

Another very simple idea for young children is to place a few small balls of clay on a board and allow them to roll them out so that the balls become strips and join up with one another. Very interesting patterns are formed in this manner. These shapes can then be fired and mounted permanently on a board to form a contemporary picture. Pendants can also be made from clay balls.

Tip: If tiles, such as door numbers, are to be placed outside where they may come into contact with frosty conditions, leave unglazed and fire to a high biscuit temperature of at least $1080°C$ ($1976°F$) or alternatively use a high-temperature stoneware glaze, firing to at least $1260°C$ ($2300°F$).

N.B. For the 'golden wedding' tile a buff clay and a honey glaze (Podmores P. 2140) was used to give a golden effect.

If extra bright colours are required on the tiles, glaze the tile after biscuit firing and then carefully paint on the oxides or stains before glaze firing — but ensure that there is no glaze left on the back of the tile, otherwise it will stick to the shelves in the kiln.

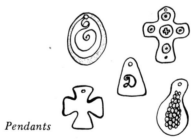

Pendants

Wrap pots: The wrap pot is a very effective type of pot for the beginner potter to make and involves one of the easiest techniques. To make one, roll out the clay as previously described and cut two straight edges as shown in the diagram. Remove surplus clay and put aside. Next take a tube (this can be the cardboard inside of a toilet roll, a card centre cut from a carpet roll or even a tin can) and wrap a piece of newspaper around it, tucking in the ends where possible. Then lay the wrapped tube on the clay and roll the clay around the tube. Scuff the edges where the clay meets and join them with a little slip (i.e. clay and water mixed to a thin paste). The surplus clay flange can be left as a decoration or trimmed off

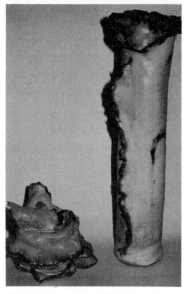

Wrap pots with pinched edges decorated with oxides

Wrap pots decorated with copper oxide and stoneware glazed

if preferred. Whilst the tube is still inside the clay, stand it upright on one of the spare pieces of rolled-out clay and cut around it to form a base for the pot. Again, scuff the edges and join with slip. Smooth the outside of the join to ensure there will be no leakages when the pot is finished. Now remove the tube and with a quick twist remove the newspaper from the pot. At this point it is a good idea to smooth the inside of the pot with a long stick or modelling tool — particularly around the seams (a slightly wet paintbrush is useful for this purpose). Lastly, thin the rim of the pot or trim it and smooth it if preferred and then texture and decorate the pot as desired.

Using this basic technique many different types of pottery can be made, such as:

a a simple single vase as described above.

b multiple vases of different heights joined to one base.

c 'tree' pots — the outer surface textured to simulate bark and the top rim torn — these are lovely pots for children to make and look very effective if branches are added and little birds made to sit on them.

Tree Pots — wrap method

SLAB WARE

d log pots — these are tree pots, but with two closed ends and a hole made in the side for posies — the pot is laid on its side, of course.

e half-logs with flowers or little animals sitting on them — these are purely ornaments.

f a tall wrap pot with coils added to the rim to form a neck — this makes a nice wine bottle.

g jugs — form a lip in the rim and add a handle (the making of these will be described later in Ch. 7).

h pencil tidies — a group of cylindrical pots of different heights joined together.

i mugs and tankards — cylinders with handles added, but with special attention paid to the smoothness of the inside of the cylinder.

Ideas for children: They will enjoy making forts, cannons, totem poles, trees, etc.

Fairy castle — three wrap pots on a hollow rock — oxides applied over white earthenware glaze

Pencil-tidy

Candle log pots

Leaf dishes: This most attractive form of pottery is quite simple to make though, unfortunately, it tends to be rather seasonal as the best leaves for this purpose are not normally available until late summer. I find that the larger leaves such as sycamore, maple, wild rhubarb, dock and fig leaves are amongst the best for table dishes, whilst the smaller leaves such as lime and beech are ideal for decoration as additions to larger pots, such as the tall wrap pot. For the really large hors d'oeuvres dishes the bracken fern makes a splendid pattern.

Leaves: Sycamore (left) and broad-leaved lime

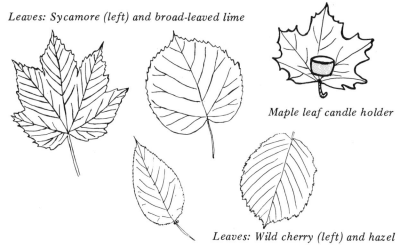

Maple leaf candle holder

Leaves: Wild cherry (left) and hazel

Method:

a Roll out the clay to an even thickness, using guides and cloth.

b Remove the base stalk from the leaf and lay it on the rolled-out clay (veins side downwards).

c Using the rolling pin, roll the leaf gently into the clay so that it becomes embedded into the clay.

d With a needle or sharp-pointed tool cut around the shape of the leaf.

e Now remove the clay and leaf from the cloth and gently pinch the edges

Leaf made with red clay, glazed with earthenware honey glaze

Sycamore and bracken leaves

of the clay leaf. Try to bend it gently inwards as you do this.

f Place the clay and leaf gently on a board and make some small 'sausages' of clay which should be placed under the upturned edges so that they are provided with support.

g At this stage – and only now – gently peel the leaf from the clay. A perfect imitation of the real leaf should be revealed in the clay and you have your leaf dish!

h If you wish to decorate the clay leaf with stains, do so carefully, picking out the veins and edges – do not paint the leaf all over.

i After biscuit firing, use a simple basic glaze (such as transparent or white opaque glaze) which will not distract from the beautiful lines of nature. An alternative effect is not to paint the dish at all but just to glaze it with one glaze and then splash it with a second glaze – e.g., a turquoise glaze over a white. If the veins are to be picked out with oxides, I find the best are copper carbonate and iron oxide (red).

There are many variations of this tecnhique. Multiple leaf dishes are most effective and are very useful as they can be quite large. To make these, place several leaves on the clay slab and cut around the multiple outline. Sets of leaf dishes of the same variety but different sizes make lovely presents and are always welcome. Quite tall pots can be made from leaf-shaped slabs and, of course, small leaves can be used purely as a three-dimensional decoration. Remember, too, that leaves with pronounced veins can make very attractive designs on traditional pots if pressed into the surface whilst the clay is still damp.

Ideas for children: Generally children find these leaf dishes quite easy to make, and they also like to make pendants and necklaces from leaves. There is much fun, too, to be had in the actual searching for suitable leaves – however, do use them whilst they are fresh as they are not much use once they become dried out. They will usually keep for a few days if sealed in a damp polythene bag.

Masks: These can have a sculptural quality and be used purely in a decorative sense, or they can just be fun for children to play with – particularly around Hallowe'en or November 5th.

Method:

a Make a tracing or drawing of the mask to be made.

b Lay drawing on to a fairly large piece of rolled-out clay.

c With a needle, cut through the main features and outline of the mask.

d Lay the clay mask over a prepared paper hump made out of screwed-up newspaper which has been slightly dampened. The mask can then be pressed and modelled into shape to give sunken eyes and high cheek-bones, etc.

e Leave to dry slowly.

f When biscuit-fired to a normal temperature of 960°C (1760°F), glaze in an earthenware white opaque glaze, paint on top of the unfired glaze with brightly coloured stains and oxides and glaze fire to a temperature of 1080°C (1976°F).

Mask

Bag pot

Bag Pots: A bag pot is a very exciting and challenging pot to make as no two ever look alike and one never knows how the next one will turn out — it all depends on the fall of the sand and the punch of the fist! It is a fairly difficult type of pot to master, but a lot of fun — or frustration — can be had trying.

Method:

a Roll out a fairly large piece of clay.

b Fill a strong paper bag, or preferably a polythene bag, with sand, and tie the top of it with string or a piece of wire. As this is to be the former for your pot, select the size you require carefully.

c Wrap the clay around the bag of sand by placing the bag in the centre of the clay slab and drawing up the walls from the front and back, pinching the side edges — rather like a Cornish pasty. You may need to cut a few 'V' section (as in needlework) in order to gather up the neck satisfactorily.

d When the edges have been joined give the bag, now surrounded by clay, a few gentle punches — an interesting shape will begin to form. Do this gently or the clay seams will burst.

e When the required shape has been achieved, leave this bag alone for a few hours — just long enough for it to firm up (if you leave it too long the clay bag will crack as it shrinks over the sand-bag). When set, untie the neck of the sand-bag and pour the sand contents into a spare container for use next time. The inside bag may then be easily removed.

f If you have not already done so, gently texture the clay bag with a broken stick and leave it to dry very slowly.

These bag pots make superb vases — particularly for wild grasses and leaf and twig displays.

Balloon pots: This is another idea using a similar technique to that used when making bag pots, but using an inflated balloon.

Wrap the clay around the balloon and make your own variations on a theme — for example:

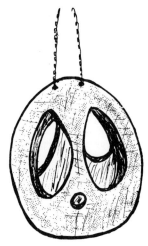

Hanging planter made around a balloon

a A hanging plant pot — cut out holes in the sides of the walls for the plants to hang through and make two holes in the top for the hanging wires.

b A dachshund dog — use a long balloon and add legs, tail, nose and ears.

c A Humpty-Dumpty — use the whole balloon and paint on the face etc.

d A piggy-bank — add ears, nose and tail and make a slot and a hole to remove the money from — it's such a shame to break it to get at the money!

f An elephant — a slightly more difficult animal to fashion, but worth trying.

g A fish — just add fins and tail and a coil for the mouth, and texture the scales.

The important factor when making any of these pots is to remember to burst the balloon before the clay dries — the best time is at the leather-hard stage, which is when the clay has slightly hardened but has not begun to shrink very much as it dries.

Simple hanging basket: This is one of the easiest pots to make.
Method:

a Roll out a piece of clay about the size of a large dinner plate.

b Lay the clay over a hump — e.g. a soup dish covered with a piece of newspaper or a hump of screwed-up paper.

c Press down gently and smooth edges.

d Make three holes in the rim, in the form of a triangle, for hanging thongs.

e Leave to dry and then lift off gently from the former.

f Smooth lightly with a damp sponge and paint on any designs with oxides.

g Biscuit fire and glaze. If to be left outside, biscuit fire high and leave unglazed. Remember the glaze on the pot prevents porosity so will stop the pot from leaking when the plants are watered. Outside, of course, this does not matter so much.

Cactus simulated brick pots: These are very attractive and look well on brick walls and in corners.

Method:

a Roll out clay and cut out a three-sided shape with two straight sides and one random edge.

b Cut out more slabs to form walls of different heights.

c Using a pointed wooden tool, draw on the walls a simulated brick design and then build up the walls, ensuring that the joins are well scuffed and that small rolls of clay are used to hinge the walls for strength.

d Using the pinch-pot method, make a little animal or sleeping Mexican for a corner decoration to the pot. To make the Mexican, a simple way is to make a thick coil, split it in two half way down to form his legs, and make a large Mexican hat by the pinch-pot method. Bend the legs to form knees and place the hat tilted forwards over the thick part of the coil. You will then have your sleeping Mexican under his hat with only his knees protruding. Alternatively, make a small tortoise.

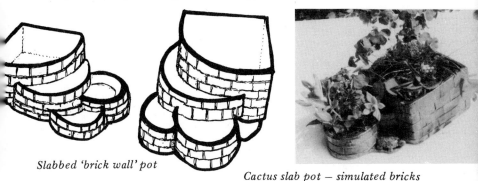

Slabbed 'brick wall' pot

Cactus slab pot — simulated bricks

Traditional slab pots and boxes: The traditional slab pot is, in my opinion, one of the more difficult forms of pottery, and it should not be attempted until the potter has acquired a complete awareness and understanding of clay and properties.

Method:

a Before commencing to make a slab pot it is necessary to calculate the exact size of the walls, taking into account the thickness of the clay and the position of the walls to the base — i.e., whether they will rest on or alongside the base. Think about it and you will realize how important these calculations are!

b Using a grogged clay, roll out a large slab to a determined thickness. (If the clay is not already grogged then a fine grog or sieved builders' sand can be added at the kneading stage — this will give strength to the clay and make the slabs firmer and so easier to build.)

c Cut the slabs to the measurements already decided upon and place them on a board, taking care not to distort them.

Slabbed casserole

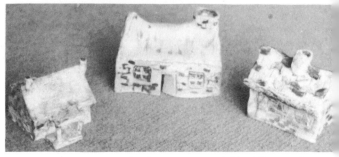

Slab pot with 'tenmoku' stoneware glaze

Cottages

Sculpture — two slabbed jigsaw pieces

Plug and socket — stoneware

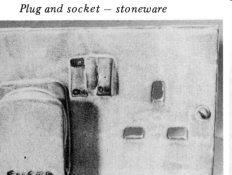

Triple slabbed vase with torn edges

Slab pot with slabbed strips added

d Leave them to dry for a short while so that they will harden a little. They will then retain their shape and not sag when joined together.

e Join the slabs of clay, ensuring that the edges to be joined are well scuffed (a broken lollipop stick is ideal for this) and wetted with slip. Press well together, and hold a small board up against the slab being joined as a support. Make some very thin rolls of clay and press gently into the joins of the seams to form a hinge. These rolls should be smoothed in to give a bevelled finish. Not only do these coils give a nicely finished appearance but they also give strength.

f When the pot has been constructed it may be left as it is with the rim smoothed and finished, or a neck may be coiled on to creat a bottle or a lamp base. If making a lid, add coils of clay to form a lip on the inside of the pot, or make it larger so that it fits neatly on top with a coiled ridge inside of the lid.

g When finishing a slab pot always bevel the sharp edges on the outside of the pot — this gives the professional finish.

h If patterns are to be incised or pressed into the slabbed walls of the pot, this should be done before construction as sometimes the action of pressing in causes the clay to stretch. The adjustment can be made by trimming before construction.

As previously mentioned, the technique of slabbing is quite difficult but practice does make perfect so *do* persevere — it really is worth while! *Ideas for children*: Although some slab work is fairly intricate, there are many simple ideas that will appeal to children and I shall describe below several ideas using slabbed clay that children may use around Christmas time. These ideas were my contribution to a teachers' handbook called *Christmas Exchange* published in 1981, but I feel they could be usefully reprinted in this book.

a Christmas wind-chimes
b Christmas mobiles
c Yule log
d Christmas cracker
e Nativity figures
f Christmas tiled panel

Christmas Wind-chimes Make paper templates of two sizes of, for example, Christmas trees, holly leaves, bells etc. Roll out clay, place template on clay and cut round to make tiles. Make as many as are required, and pierce a hole at top and centre of base of trees, leaves, bells etc.

Decorate tiles with oxides and then biscuit fire. Glaze, transparent or white opaque. Alternatively, these tiles may be painted with gloss paint after biscuit firing.

Using appropriate thread, shapes can be balanced in different ways and suspended from ceiling. Placed in a draught, these chimes will make a pretty tinkling sound.

Christmas mobiles Roll out clay thinly and cut out star shapes with a slot in each so that if two are slotted together a snowflake shape is formed. Pierce a hole in one of the star shapes and when fired glue together for hanging. Make as many star shapes as required for mobile and hang with spring wire.

These can be glazed all white, opaque glaze (P. 2116), or varied with oxides, applied before biscuit firing and then glazed (P. 2116).

Yule log Roll out clay between two slats and wrap around a tube covered with newspaper – red clay is best for this, though grey may be used and coloured with iron oxide before biscuit firing. Texture clay with a rough stick to look like a log and leave each end rugged or add on a base with 'log circles'. Make a little robin (this may be solid) and a few holly leaves if desired. Paint holly leaves with copper carbonate.

Biscuit fire and then paint on white opaque glaze (P. 2116) fairly thickly where snow effect required. Use red gloss paint for any holly berries and robin's breast after log is glaze fired.

Christmas cracker Make as for Yule log but this time use grey clay. Cut cracker in half when removed from tube in a zigzag fashion to give torn effect. Paint with colours before biscuit firing, or, if bright colours are desired, after glaze has been applied.

Make pendants and small animal objects, as presents, to go inside cracker.

Nativity figures Figures are formed around a simple cone base – as shown in the illustration. For the arms, use thick coils, and for the head, two thumb pots joined together to form an egg shape, or the head may be solid if small. For the hair, soft clay pushed through a coarse sieve. Thumb pots for the hats, and for crowns, shawls and wings, clay rolled out flat and cut to shape. Material-like folds can be created by adding thin coils and smoothing to shape.

Christmas wind-chimes

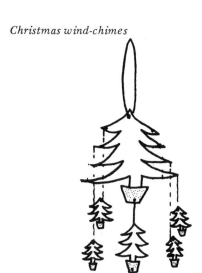

Having made the figures, paint with oxides and stains, biscuit fire 960°C (1760°F) and glaze with a white opaque glaze — e.g. Podmores P. 2116. Glaze fire 1080°C (1976°F). Alternatively if brighter colours are required the oxides and stains may be painted on top of the glaze before firing. If the figures are made with red clay they are best left unfired, burnished, or glazed with a honey glaze — e.g. Podmore's P. 2140.

Christmas tiled panel Tiles should be made individually and fixed with adhesive to a piece of hardboard or plywood to form the panel. Tiles should be made from clay (grey preferably) rolled out between two slats to give evenness of thickness and cut out with a tile cutter or by using a knife and ruler. They should have three or four grooves guaged into the back of them to ensure flat drying. These grooves also have the advantage of assisting the tiles to stick to the board as they contain the adhesive.

Pictures can be inscribed with a pointed tool and painted with oxides and stains, or be created by laying cut out clay shapes on to tiles and joining the two layers with slip. This method gives the tiles a raised effect. If really bright colours are required, paint stains and oxides on top of the glaze before it is fired.

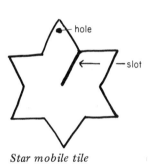

Star mobile tile

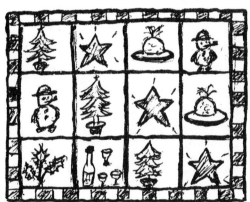

Christmas tiled panel

Nativity figures — wrapping clay around a cone

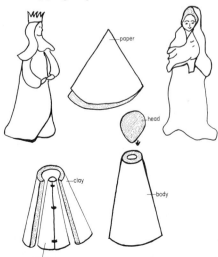

45

5 Coiled Pottery

The coiling method was the way in which primitive man first made his pots, and this technique was the forerunner of the throwing of pots on a turntable, or potter's wheel, as we now call it. The great advantage of the technique of coiling is that very few tools are needed and it is easy to do almost anywhere. Coiling is the most versatile technique of all for making pots of all shapes and sizes, and it is extremely exciting to do. Sometimes the large variety of possibilities may seem rather confusing, as, too, are the many ways in which a coil pot may be made. With practice, pots can be coiled to a size which would take many years to equal using a wheel. For many hundreds of years the people of Greece and Cyprus made huge coil pots as wine vats. They were so large that three or four people could stand inside them. These pots are also to be found in southern Spain in the wine-making areas.

PREPARATION
At first the most difficult part of making a coil pot is the actual rolling of the coils, but this becomes easier with practice. However, the following tips will certainly prove useful:

a Ensure the clay is fairly soft and well kneaded.

b Make several 'sausages' of clay approximately 15 cm. long x 4 cm. thick (6in. x 1½ in.).

c Find a large table top with a smooth surface (preferably wooden).

d Place a sausage of clay on the table, spread the fingers of each hand and roll the sausage over the surface of the table, pressing gently with the fingers as you roll (DO NOT use the palms of the hands at all). Move the fingers gently along the sausage as you roll the clay in a full 360° turn — DO NOT rock the clay or a pleat will form which will trap air and air and also cause the coil to flatten.

e When the coil has lengthened to around 30 cm. (12 in.) break apart and put coil aside whilst you roll the other to the required thickness. To begin with I would suggest a thickness of around 1 cm. ($\frac{3}{8}$in.). Always work fingers from the middle of the coil and move gently outwards.

f When seven or eight coils, to the required thickness, have been made, put them aside and cover with polythene to prevent them drying out.

g Find a piece of plywood or hardboard (about 15-20 cm. (6-8 in.) square, and if you have a turntable place the board on it.

h If you are in any doubt as to the exact shape you intend making your

46

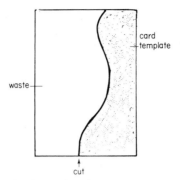

Card template for a coiled pot.

pot, it is advisable to make a template from a piece of cardboard to offer to the side of your pot as it grows – this will help to keep it symmetrical and help the end product to look like the pot as planned.

METHOD

a Having made your coils, roll out a piece of clay to about 1 cm. ($\frac{3}{8}$ in.) thick (i.e. the same thickness as your coils) and cut it round using a tile cutter, drawing around a round object such as a jar or tin, or using compasses – about 10 cm. (4 in.) in diameter. Remember to inscribe any form of identification on the bottom side of this circular base of the pot before you commence building.

Place a coil of clay to form a ring on the clay base and join the two ends together (tip – always make the coils slightly shorter than you think you need them, as the clay will stretch as you apply the coils. Keeping them shorter lessens the chance of overstretching and which would cause the pot to sag.)

b The outer and inner surface of the coils must be smoothed gently to fill the gap between coil and base. Successive coils are added and the surface of each coil must be rubbed gently to form a join with the wall beneath. Do not press down on the coils – the pot must be allowed to *grow* and pressing down will cause bulging of the walls. If a tall pot is to be built, it is a good idea to put the pot aside to harden slightly (say for about half an hour) when 15-20 cm. (6-8 in.) has been built in order to allow the walls to strengthen and not sag with their own weight. (Note – slip or water should NOT be used in the coiling process as it will soften the clay too much). It is sometimes a temptation to build the coils in a long spiral – this is not advisable as the pot will usually get out of control very quickly and end up lop-sided!

c As the pot grows it will almost certainly need to be widened and narrowed. The way to do this is as follows:
Widening – place the coils so that they slightly overlap the wall beneath, in an outward direction.

47

Tall coil pot — stoneware

Coil pot in red clay —
glazed in earthenware honey

Coil pot with design
painted in oxides

Stoneware coil pot

Narrowing — place the coils so that they lie slightly inside of the wall beneath.

Remember to use the template from time to time to check the rate of widening and narrowing.

d When you have finished the basic building of the pot, check to see that the rim is flat and even — and level. To check that it is indeed level, place a small board across it and stand back to look at it — you will soon see if it leans downhill. If it does, correct the level by adding a thin coil where it is uneven. It is usually a good idea, visually, to have the finished rim of the pot thinner than the main walls. The observer's eye will usually see the rim first and if the rim is fine then the effect is that the whole pot is fine. The converse is also true, of course, so if you have made a delicate pot do ensure that the rim is delicate.

c Before finally smoothing the outside of the pot or adding any form of inscribed or sprigged decoration, do check its overall shape with the template — or anyway check that it is symmetrical. If the shape of the pot is not even, it is a good idea to gently reshape the pot by tapping the outside walls with a flat ruler or stick. Do this very lightly and gently, turning the pot as you do it.

f When satisfied with the final shape of the pot, smooth the outside with a damp sponge and add any form of pattern. Usually beginners' coil pots look best incised or textured and it is wise not to make first pots taller than 40 cm (16 in.).

48

Owls — pinch pots

Collage of eight tiles depicting African dancers

Three thrown bowls

Triple thrown pot

As mentioned earlier, do not try to make a coil pot all in one go – make it in stages. It is often a good idea to make two or three pots at the same time. Whilst one pot is drying off the next one may be built.

N.B. Do remember to smooth the inside of the pot as you build it, as this can be almost impossible to do once the neck is formed.

An alternative way to start a coil pot is to use a pinch pot as a base. Personally, I do not like this method, but if you do try it, remember to flatten the base or the pot will rock as you make it. However, if for some reason you want the pot to have a rounded bottom I would suggest it should be rested in either a coiled circle of clay or on a fairly thick dry sponge.

Drying: Allow coil pots to dry very slowly. After finishing it is often a good idea to allow the pot to sit in a large damp polythene bag for two or three days before allowing it to dry naturally in the air – this will allow it to acquire an all-over dampness and so dry evenly when exposed.

RECIPES

Agate Coiled Pottery: This can be made quite simply by using two different coloured clays such as red and grey and coiling alternate colours. Alternatively, to make really pretty coloured pots, make up several small batches of different coloured clays by kneading into the soft grey clay a body stain or an oxide. Make up separate batches of coloured coils from the coloured clays and use them in sequence to build the pot. The smoothing action on the wall surface will cause the colours to blend and when glazed with a transparent earthenware glaze will produce some really fascinating coloured effects. Try the following: Red and grey clay and three batches of grey clay stained with blue stain, copper carbonate and manganese dioxide.

Fruit Bowls or Rose Bowls: These look very nice coiled but look best if a foot is coiled onto them. Add one or two coils to the rounded base and smooth them so that they look a part of the main body of the pot. Alternatively, coil a separate base stand and add it to the base of the bowl using a thin coil and scuffing the two edges to be joined – here a little slip is necessary to effect a strong join.

Coiled red clay bowl, burnished and carved, insides glazed with earthenware 'honey' glaze

Coiled bottle – stoneware glaze

49

COILED POTTERY

Lamp Bases: This is a very popular form of coil pot, but do remember to make a hole at the base of the pot for the wire and check the size of the fitting for the neck. There are various types available in shops nowadays — the metal variety that must be fixed with an Araldite type adhesive, the cork fitting or a wooden wedge is often most satisfactory. Whatever it is, it must not rock when the lamp and shade are fitted! Remember that clay shrinks when fired, so allow for this when measuring the fitting.

Lidded Pots: If making lidded pots, remember to make the lid at the same time as you make the pot — do not make the lid after the pot has dried because it will not fit! Different clays shrink at varying rates, but generally from beginning to end — i.e. from the wet clay stage to the finished glazed pot — a shrinkage of between 8-10% should be expected.

Sculptural Shapes: Large sculptural models such as birds and animals can be made very satisfactorily using the coiling method. Heads and busts, too, are made from a coiled base — though usually over an armature.

IDEAS FOR CHILDREN

Generally children find traditional coil pottery quite difficult, so it is better to start them off using coils in another way. Below are a few suggestions:

Coiled Models: For these, use a slightly grogged clay, or if you only have a smooth clay add a little sieved sand or fine grog. The model figures can be made by pressing coils of equal length together at the middle to form the body, spreading the ends of the coils to form the legs, or arms and legs, of the figure and adding a ball of clay (which has been made hollow by pressing a finger into it) to make the head. If it is to be an animal add another thin coil for its tail, and if hair is to be added this can be made by pushing soft clay through a coarse metal sieve. If the figures are to be of the human variety they can be dressed in cloaks and clothes made from rolled-out clay and made to sit on rocks (hollow) or seats. Children are very imaginative indeed once these ideas are presented to them. This technique can be great fun, too, when explored more thoroughly by adults — e.g. two tramps sitting on a park bench, crinoline ladies and circus clowns — even a Father Christmas!

Brick Pots: These are made in a very similar way to coiled pottery. The main difference is the actual building of the pots. The coils are made in the same way and a base rolled out. The difference occurs in that the coils are cut up into brick-shaped pieces (say 2 cm. x 1 cm. x 1 cm.) (1 in. x ½ in. x ½ in.) and the walls are built in the same 'broken joint' fashion that a real brick wall is built. However, instead of cement, it is useful to use slip (clay and water). The slip is applied between the bricks and the *inside* only of the brick walls is smoothed. These brick-built pots can be made in any shape and make lovely wishing wells, houses, money boxes, ash trays and, of course, the basis for forts and castles. Once again, the imagination can run happily along. These brick pots look especially good if made with red clay, painted with little spots of blue and green stains between the bricks to look like mosses and then, after biscuit firing, glazed with a white opaque earthenware glaze (e.g. Podmore's P. 2116). Even very young children find this technique quite easy, and if there is more than one child doing claywork it is a good idea for one child to make the bricks whilst the other builds. To them it will seem a similar activity to the building bricks they are familiar with such as 'Lego' and 'Bettabuilder'.

Finally, remember that coils can be used decoratively as well as for the actual building process. Fine coils make very good filigree decoration — particularly on plant holders.

Church made of clay 'bricks' and thatched with clay which has been extruded through a kitchen sieve

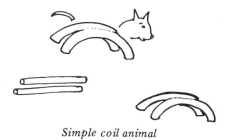

Simple coil animal

6 Pottery made from Plaster Moulds

The art of making pottery from moulds, using the press moulding or the slip moulding techniques, dates back many hundreds of years and was used by the early Staffordshire potters for making what is termed 'flat-ware' — e.g. platters, shallow dishes and plates. These dishes were decorated using various different techniques such as slip trailing, marbling, inscribing and appliqué. All that is needed for these techniques is plaster moulds (I shall describe quite simply how one can make these), some clay or slip, decorating colours (oxides and stains) and a few simple tools.

Pottery made from moulds was the basis of mass-production pottery — and still is today, for it is the cheapest and fastest way of making similar and almost identical pieces of pottery — i.e. sets of pottery. The techniques described in this chapter are particularly useful for people in the early stages of pottery-making, for without having acquired particular skills the hobby potter may produce many very acceptable pieces of pottery ware and also make many variations on a theme.

THE MOULD

Pottery moulds are almost always made from plaster of Paris. They may be purchased, in their many varieties, from pottery suppliers or made by the individual potter to suit his or her own requirments. Bought moulds vary from very simple ones such as those for a round dish to the very intricate moulds used, for example, by people making chess sets or tea services. However, as the simple mould is so easy to make I do recommend the hobby potter to have a go at making one as so much can be learned and a great deal of fun experienced.

There are various ways of making moulds, and I shall describe in this chapter some of the most common methods used. However, before doing so I feel I should explain something about the material to be used. Plaster is not expensive if purchased sensibly, and if a few basic rules are observed no problems should occur.

Plaster of Paris: Various forms of plaster are available and all can be used to make moulds — however, the best and easiest to use is plaster of Paris. Some potters do use builder's plaster but this needs to be experimented with as different types vary considerably. Fortunately plaster is still one of the cheapest of all craft materials and is indeed, one of the most useful. However, it is also one of the messiest materials to work with if not

handled correctly. When buying and using plaster note the following advice:
Purchasing in quantity: Buy plaster (a potter's plaster is best) from a
pottery supplier in large quantities — that is to say, as large a quantity as
you can conveniently store and use (e.g. 10 Kg. or 25 Kg.) (22 lb. or
56 lb.) Do not buy small quantities from chemists or ironmongers as
this is an extremely expensive way of purchasing. If you are attempting
to use builder's plaster then this can usually be obtained from your local
builder's merchant, but do check that it is finely ground and not lumpy!
Storage: Plaster needs to be kept *absolutely dry* and is best stored in a
dustbin or plastic clip-on type storage bin. Always keep a scoop in the bin
with the plaster for ladling it out, as plaster — particularly clay which is
to be fired — must be protected from contamination by other materials.
Contamination will usually cause the clay to explode when fired.
Dangers: Plaster can cause all sorts of havoc if allowed to go down sinks,
for it can block pipes and drains. Therefore, if you must wash plaster-
contaminated utensils at a sink ALWAYS ensure that the cold tap is left
running for at least 10 minutes in order to wash away all the particles of
plaster from the sink and pipes. If possible it is preferable to keep a
bucket handy for preliminary hand washing and then empty the contents
on the ground outside when you have finished.
Mixing: Before mixing the plaster, prepare everything you need, including
the frame which will surround the mould, made from interlocking boards.
Also decide what you intend to do with any plaster that may be left
over — it may be useful to make a simple hump mould from a plastic basin
or it may make a plaster slab for drying clay on. In either case you will
need to have made your preparations for plaster, once mixed with water,
has a *very* short life before it sets.

Pour into a bowl a quantity of water that is about equal in volume to
the amount of plaster you require. With the scoop, sprinkle plaster into
the water until it begins to peak above the surface of the water — like the
Swiss Alps! Approximately 1 Kg. (2 lb.) of plaster to ½ litre (1 pint) of
water will achieve this. At this stage leave it undisturbed for about one
minute and then stir it together gently with the hand, in a circular motion
— until thoroughly mixed. After a minute or so it will begin to thicken,
and when it becomes a thick creamy texture it is ready to be poured into
the mould. It must be used quickly when it reaches this stage as it will
become solid very rapidly. Remember that once plaster has begun to
thicken, the process cannot be slowed down!

PLASTER SLABS

Before moving on to the techniques of making various types of moulds
I feel mention should be made of the value of making plaster slabs for use
in the drying out of used clay that has been soaked. As plaster absorbs
damp more quickly than any other material it is an ideal medium for use
with the drying of clay, and a plaster slab is best for this purpose. To make
slabs, you will need to set up a framework by laying four pieces of wood

on a board covered with polythene so that they form a rectangular frame. Fix the pieces of wood in position with clay and use clay to fill any gaps through which the wet plaster may escape. Mix the plaster with water and pour it into the framework to a depth of about 5 cm. (2 in.). If it is poured while fairly liquid it will level itself out quite quickly, though it is a good idea to pat the surface gently all over to remove the air bubbles. As an alternative to making up a frame for this job, I have found it useful to obtain an old drawer and, having broken the corner joints, screw them up again so that they can easily be unscrewed when releasing the plaster slab when set. Do allow the slab to dry completely before using it as a drying-out slab, or as a base on which to knead moist clay.

MAKING A MOULD

1 First decide what form the retaining walls of the mould are to take. There are various options:

a   An ordinary plastic bowl or container.

b   A strip of old lino or stout cardboard set on a polythene-covered board.

c   A set of four adjustable boards which can be adjusted to any rectangular or square shape, as required — these are also placed on a board covered with a sheet of polythene.

N.B. Remember to seal all gaps with wet clay to prevent any wet plaster oozing out!

2 Make a solid mound of clay to the shape you wish your final dish or bowl to be and place it upside down in the centre of the retaining vessel. Smooth it well with a fine sponge until it is as perfect as it can possibly be — remember that any imperfections will be repeated on any future castings. Check that there is a gap of at least 5 cm. (2 in.) between the clay mound and the retaining walls. Then, having mixed sufficient plaster to cover the mould and allow approximately 7 cm. (2½ in.) thickness of plaster above the hump, pour the wet plaster into the framework and allow the plaster to set and cool. Note — the plaster will heat up as it sets. This is due to a chemical process that is quite fascinating — particularly to children, as they can see no heat applied. When set — and it is advisable to allow an hour or so to elapse — turn the plastic bowl upside down and press the plaster mould out gently onto your hand, before laying it on a board. If a framework is used, release it, remove the plaster mould and place it on a board. Next, carefully pull out the clay hump from the centre of the mould and wash the mould gently. Smooth off any sharp edges with a WOODEN tool and allow the plaster mould to dry thoroughly before using it to make your sets of dishes — press-mould fashion. Do not dry plaster moulds over direct heat.

MAKING A PRESS-MOULDED DISH

1 Roll out a lump of clay that has first been wedged and kneaded well, to a thickness of approximately 1 cm ($\frac{3}{8}$ in.). The overall size of the slab of clay should be at least 7 cm (2½ in.) larger than the mould.

2   Check that there are no air bubbles in the clay – if you find some, pierce them with a sharp needle to release the air and smooth over with your finger. Leave the flat slab of clay on the cloth it has been rolled out on and use it whilst it is still damp (it does not need to dry to a firm state as in slab pot building).

3   Check that the mould to be used is clean and wipe the interior surface with a slightly damp sponge to ensure that any foreign particles are removed. This process also removes any powdery surface from the mould that might contaminate the clay that is to be pressed on to it.

4   Gently place the slab of clay over the mould and remove the cloth. The cloth will usually leave an imprint on the clay surface but this will be easy to remove as the clay is eased gently into the cavity of the mould with a damp sponge. Great care must be taken at this stage in the pressing of the clay into the mould. Gently lift the edges of the clay as you sponge it into position to prevent the clay in the mould being stretched. Remember it needs to move into place, not stretch! If it is stretched it will be thinner in places, particularly the corners, and consequently weaker. It sometimes helps to trim the excess clay at this stage, leaving only a small margin – do this with a wooden tool or lollipop stick, as it is less likely to damage the surface of the mould. (A metal tool or knife is likely to chip the mould and so leave small pieces of plaster embedded in the damp clay which cause problems when the pot is fired.) Always be on the lookout for any small flecks of plaster in the clay, for they really can damage a good pot – hence the importance of caring for a mould and using it correctly.

5   To finish the edge of the dish whilst in the mould, it is best to cut with a horizontal action using a flat wooden tool such as a lollipop stick. As you cut, ensure that you do not pull the clay away from the mould. Once all the excess clay has been removed, the edge and inside of the dish may be smoothed over with a soft damp sponge.

6   Alternatively, if a shallow mould is being used it is possible to leave the excess clay on the edge of the mould so that it gives the bowl a rim. However, it will need to be trimmed neatly and sponged to give it a smooth finish.

7   The clay must remain in the mould for about two hours before it is removed. During this time the moisture from the clay is absorbed by the plaster mould, causing the clay to shrink and therefore be removed quite easily. I find the best method of removal is to place a board over the mould and then invert the mould. The mould can then be lifted from the dish which is left upside down on the board ready for its final drying. (The process is rather like turning out a jelly from its mould.) In this position the dish is unlikely to warp as the rim is firmly in position on the board and the dish will receive even exposure during its final drying time. However, do not allow this to be too rapid – it is a good idea to place a flat piece of polythene lightly over the dish during the first 12 hours or so of drying in order to prevent any surface cracks.

Moulded dishes — slip decorated

Bottle and wine jug made by joining two press moulds

Owls made using press moulds

Decoration: Whilst the dish is still inside the mould awaiting its first two hours' drying time it may be decorated in a variety of ways — e.g. slip trailing, feathering or marbling, sgraffito or simply painting a pattern with stains or oxldes. These techniques and others are explained more fully in Chapter 9 which deals with the many various techniques of decoration.

IDEAS

Hors d'oeuvre dishes: made by joining two or three, or more, together side by side or in a 'daisy' fashion.

Bottles: Join two together with slip, rim to rim, flatten the base and then coil a neck.

Wine jugs: These can be made in the same way as bottles but my making a lip for pouring and adding a handle (see Chapter 7 for pulling handles).

Animals: The method can be used for making models such as animals — e.g. a tortoise or turtle — the dish (an oval one) being its shell and then four leg stumps and a head added. These may be solid if not thicker than your finger, but even so it is a good ideal to drill a small hole with a rounded tool or needle to prevent any explosion of the solid mass.

Dish on a stand: Add a foot ring by rolling out a coil and smoothing it

onto the base of the dish. With care this technique can look quite professional and the whole dish will look as one, the join being unnoticed.
Hanging planter: Decorate or texture the outside of the dish and hang it in a string macramé holder. An alternative way of making a planter is by using two fairly deep dish moulds, joining them as for a bottle and cutting out holes in the upper sides of the pot at the leather-hard stage (these holes provide openings for the plants to trail through). Remember to pierce two small holes in the top of the planter so that a wire may be threaded through for hanging it up.

N.B. When joining the rims of two press moulds together, do ensure that the surface to be joined are well scored and joined with a thick slip (clay and water). After pressing the two edges together the seams should be smoothed over so that it is impossible to see the joins. It this is not done satisfactorily the pots will not look good and it is possible that the seams will open up during firing! Remember that trapped air expands during firing and so will a bad seam.

Alternative ideas for making Press Moulds: Moulds may be made quite easily from many household objects, such as plates, saucers, simple models etc. The important factor is that the shapes should be simple and not have any underlipping flanges, so making it impossible for the mould to release the former. Before pouring plaster of Paris over these simple commercially made items (e.g. those made of china, metal or plastic) remember it is first necessary to coat these objects with a solution made from green soft soap dissolved in boiling water (ratio 113 gm. to 142 ml. or 4oz. to ¼ pint) water, which should be applied with a small sponge, or alternatively a mould maker's size can be purchased from pottery suppliers, especially for this purpose. A very simple way of making a plate mould is to obtain an ordinary cardboard picnic plate and press it into a round slab of clay — the reverse way up so that it forms a mound above the clay.

Place the impressed clay and plate into a plastic washing-up bowl or an interlocking frame and pour over the plaster. When set remove the mould from the bowl or frame and gently pull out the clay and cardboard plate. When dry the mould will be ready for making all the plates you want.

The Hump Mould: This is a convex mould (i.e. the reverse of the press mould) and therefore cannot be used with slip — only with plastic clay. They are very simple indeed to make, as described below:

a   The simplest way of all to make a hump mould is to pour plaster into a plastic mixing bowl. When set it is easy to manipulate the bowl so that it releases the plaster mould.

b   Another way to make a hump mould is by using the inside of a press mould. First coat the inside of the press mould with slip, then mix sufficient plaster and water to fill the depression. Pour it in and as it is drying press a jar, a lump of wood or anything that will serve as a handle (like the stalk of a mushroom) into the plaster and hold it still for a short while until the plaster is set. This will form the handle of the mould and also provide a 'leg' for it to stand on. Smooth the surface of the plaster and leave to dry. When completely dry place the two moulds under a running tap, allowing the water to run over them. Don't forget to scrape away any plaster which is covering the clay seam between the two moulds, as the water must wash away the slip which separates them so that they will come apart. Keep the water running and gently turn the 'mushroom' mould. When separated the mould should be smoothed over with a knife and the edges bevelled. Wash the mould thoroughly and allow to dry completely before using.

Making Dishes Using the Hump Mould: Roll the clay out, as for a press mould, and drape it over the hump mould. Trim the excess clay with a wooden spatula or tool. Leave for about 20 minutes in a dry, warm atmosphere and the mould and clay should part company fairly easily. It is important that the clay is not left on the hump for longer than is necessary, as the clay will shrink as it dries and consequently the form will crack or split. Dishes made by this technique can be decorated and used to make pottery in exactly the same way as a press mould.

SLIP CASTING

This is a very quick way of making moulded pottery and is the technique used in industry. However, it is important to understand the process fairly thoroughly and to keep notes of the slip recipe you use and its absorbtion time. In this way almost identical pots may be made and so it is easy to create sets which are particularly useful in the home. Moulds that cannot easily be made by the hobby potter, as explained earlier, can be bought from pottery suppliers and, in the case of mugs, coffee sets, etc. this is the best way to produce these sets. However, I give below a simple slip-casting recipe that I find is quite suitable for pottery fired and glazed at earthenware temperatures up to 1080°C (1976°F).

Recipe:
4½ Kg. (10 lb.) china clay
4½ Kg. (10 lb.) ball clay
4 litres (7 pints) of water

Slip-cast tea-set

28 gm. (1 oz.) silicate of soda or Manger's waterglass
28 gm. (1 oz.) soda ash or washing soda
Dissolve the silicate of soda in a little very hot water and add the soda. Then mix with the water. When dissolved sprinkle the clay into the water, stirring all the time. (It is advisable to wear a mask during this process to prevent inhaling the clay dust.) When mixed, brush through an 80-mesh sieve — preferably twice — and leave to stand for a day or so before use. The soda acts as a deflocculent and keeps the clay in suspension, as well as making it more fluid. If, when you wish to use the slip, you find it too thick, add more water, mix and sieve again. On the other hand if the slip is too thin, having allowed it to stand, remove some of the surplus water resting on top of the slurry by gently pouring or syphoning it off, then stir and resieve. Remember it is always easier to thin than to thicken! For the casting, have the moulds ready — i.e. clean and dry with any joins sealed with clay to prevent leakage. Plaster moulds of the more complicated variety, having three or four sections, can be purchased from most pottery suppliers. These are ideal for slip casting but are very difficult indeed for the hobby potter to make.

Method for Making Slip Moulded Pottery
1 Check mould is bone dry and in good condition.
2 Check there are no leaky gaps, if the mould is one with several pieces; if there are, seal with clay.
3 Pour slip gently into the mould to the top.
4 Top up with more slip as the level of the slip lowers in the mould. The plaster absorbs water from the slip leaving the clay to form and thicken.
5 Watch the thickening process and time it. When the wall of the pot is the thickness you require (not less than 3 mm. ($\frac{1}{8}$ in.) thick) pour out the surplus slip and return the mould to its upright position to prevent bubbles forming on the base of the pot. Casting earthenware takes 20-30 minutes in a dry mould.
6 When the pot has dried to a cheese-hard state it should then be removed from the mould. This drying process will take two to three hours and during this time the clay form will shrink away from the plaster mould. It is advisable to time this process from the beginning to the end, for every time a really dry mould is used the timing should be the same — that is, of course, provided the consistency of the slip is correct.
7 Any further trimming with a knife or sponging of the pot - particularly around the seams - should be done when the pot is quite hard and not liable to be distorted by handling. The technical term for sponging and scraping a pot at this stage is 'fettling'.

HAMMOCK MOULDS
This is a very simple way of making a mould without the use of plaster. Obtain a greengrocer's boxwood fruit box and suspend a piece of sheeting on the inside of the box (or alternatively, for round shapes, the inside of a large bowl). Lay the rolled-out slab of clay (which has been cut to the

clay material

box frame

Moulded dishes decorated with oxides and slips

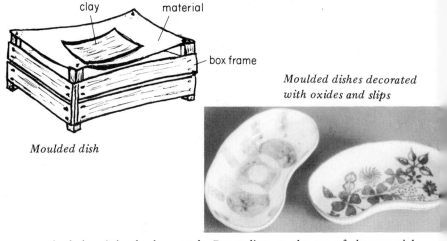

Moulded dish

required shape) in the hammock. Depending on the sag of the material and the shape of the hammock it is possible to make either deep or shallow dishes, square or round. Do not remove the mould until the shape has become leather hard or it will tend to lose its shape and may distort. This type of dish looks very good if made from a terra-cotta (red) clay and glazed only on the inside. A honey glaze such as Podmore's P. 2140 is especially suitable for this, or a marbled slip effect with just a transparent glaze over the slip. Another idea for a decorative effect is to depress textured items such as buttons, twigs, leaves, bark etc., into the clay before it is cut to shape and laid in the hammock. These shapes can then be picked out in oxides or stains or just left to 'break' through the glaze. (A white opaque glaze over a red clay is particularly effective — e.g. Podmore's P. 2116.)

SPRIGGING
Whilst discussing moulds I should mention the technique of sprigging. The sprig mould is made by making a small plaster mould in, say, a yoghurt cup, and pressing into the wet plaster a shape — e.g. a leaf, twig or button — or just carving a shape into the dry plaster. Slip is then poured into the indentation and when leather hard removed and attached to a pot with slip — thus giving a raised form of decoration. Wedgwood pottery is decorated in this manner and the raised form (as with Wedgwood) is usually of a different colour clay from the main body, giving a contrasting effect.

TILES
As a final note in this chapter I want to mention tiles. These are easily made in any shape. Make your tile, put it in a frame, pour on the plaster, remove when set and when the mould is dry make sets of tiles. Decorate with oxides or stains, and incise or add decorative pieces of clay to form a raised pattern. These can be used for walls, table tops and many other things.

7 The Potter's Wheel

The potter's wheel has a strange fascination for most people and those who master it are easily hypnotized by its 'magic'. Some people think that a pot that has not been made on a wheel is not really pottery, although this is of course not true. However, the process of forming a pot on the wheel is quite different from any other process of pottery making. It involves a skill that must be learned and practised and in the early days the beginner requires a considerable degree of patience if he or she is to succeed. However, once the 'feel' has been acquired progress is usually quite rapid, and it is rare that a person forgets the technique once success has been achieved.

CHOOSING A WHEEL

Before one can become involved in the fascinating process of throwing clay a wheel must be obtained, and this can be quite an expensive operation. There are many different types of potters' wheels available on the market today — varying in price from about a hundred pounds to about four hundred pounds, if buying a new one. Second-hand wheels are certainly worth looking out for but seem to be very scarce. An ordinary standard kick wheel is about the cheapest, then about fifty pounds dearer is a geared kick wheel which leads into the range of electrically powered wheels costing between two and four hundred pounds. Provided you are not aiming to make really large pots, such as cider jars, and are content with normal domestic ware, a portable bench wheel, which will take up to 2½ Kg. (6 lb.) of clay, is probably the most suitable choice. The Wenger's Portable Bench Wheel (model 2805 W) is a wheel I would re-commend for most people, as its height is related to that of the bench on which it is placed, so that it can be adapted for use by people of all heights. It can be easily cleaned and, if required, can be moved from place to place with minimum effort. The larger and more expensive wheels are ideal for use by those who have the experience or wish to learn to throw much larger pots. Some of the larger wheels have seats attached to them, but all are made for adult use, and young or small people usually experience physical problems. However, there is now quite a large variety of potters' wheels on the market, and in the end the choice usually comes down to personal preference and available finance.

If it is decided to buy new I would suggest a visit to a pottery show-room or exhibition where potters' wheels are being shown and demonstrated. I have listed some recommended suppliers at the end of this book. Make contact with them and see what they have to offer.

There are, of course, some people who like to make their own potter's wheel, and this is quite possible provided you have some engineering skills. The kick wheel is, perhaps, the easiest to make and plans can be purchased to assist with such a project. It is also possible to convert a kick wheel into an electric wheel, provided the motor used can be regulated to a speed that is both slow enough and fast enough. Having mentioned the kick wheel, I must explain that although many potters do, indeed, prefer to work on a kick wheel (preferably a geared one) as it is easier to control the speeds and gain sensitivity, it is not so easy to *learn* on a wheel of this type. The action of kicking one leg can be rather distracting for the beginner, and it can be diffficult to assess the best speeds required for the different stages of throwing the pot.

However, many potters do prefer to use a kick wheel for the turning of a pot — this is the final shaping and cleaning up of a leather-hard pot, a process I shall explain in more detail later on in this chapter. I shall also list points that I find particularly helpful when learning to throw a pot on a potter's wheel. However, I do not intend to delve into the finer details of the art, as many superb books have already been written on this subject, with photographs illustrating each step. In my opinion, the best book available today is John Colbeck's book, entitled *Pottery, the Technique of Throwing*, and I recommend it to any potter to keep as a 'Bible' on the subject. I have found that a useful tip for using this book is to select a page, place the opened book in a polythene bag and place it up in front of the wheel for reference. The stages are extremely easy to follow and the polythene will prevent the book being damaged by splashing clay.

USING A WHEEL

The technique of using a potter's wheel can be divided into two basic processes — throwing and turning. A pot may be thrown without the follow-up process of being turned, but a pot cannot be turned unless it has first been thrown! (The only exception to this is when a potter places a hand-built pot on the wheelhead and turns it — usually for decorative purposes.)

Tools for use with a potter's wheel

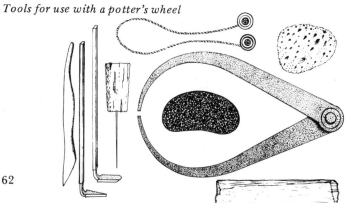

Throwing: This is the process of shaping an even mass of soft plastic clay, using one's hands, on a revolving wheelhead at varying speeds, which are controlled by the thrower.

Turning: This is a process whereby a potter pares away excess clay from a leather-hard form, using sharp tools and whilst the wheelhead is rotating slowly. The leather-hard form is usually slightly reshaped during this process.

Throwing and turning are often considered to be difficult to learn, but this is not the case provided basic rules are followed, in the correct order. As in all motor-activities regular practice is essential, but little and often will prove to be much more effective than a long stint of practice at one time. Remember the comparison to the process of learning to ride a bicycle — there are bound to be occasional falls and some will hurt more than others!

Clay: Before attempting to throw a pot, first select a suitable throwing clay — preferably one containing a small percentage of fine grog. Then, when it has been wedged and kneaded sufficiently, make it up into balls. If the intention is to make several similar pots of the same size (e.g. a set of mugs) it is advisable to weigh the clay into balls of equal weight. In this way the chance of success will be greatly improved — at least the starting-point will be with balls of clay of the same size.

Below I have listed some guidelines and given some tips to assist the beginner.

INITIAL GUIDELINES FOR THROWING A POT

1 Wedge and knead the clay and ensure it is soft enough to drop a thumb into it gently.

2 Make up balls of clay that can comfortably be encircled by both hands (usually about the size of a cricket ball) and keep in a handy place to the wheel, covered by polythene so that they do not dry out.

3 Check your tool-kit and be sure that you have in it all the tools likely to be needed during the throwing process — there is nothing worse than having to stop half way through the forming of a pot to look for something, with messy hands! Basic requirements are a bowl of water, a small sponge, a needle, a cutting wire, and some small boards for placing the pots on to dry. It is also useful to have a scraper, a pointed turning tool and a small piece of balsa wood for cleaning off the wheelhead.

4 Ensure that there is a container to collect waste water from the wheel tray if it is the type that has a drainage plug and hose.

5 Before commencing make sure that the wheelhead is DRY and clean. A piece of balsa wood scraped across the surface of the turntable will remove any damp clay and dry it at the same time.

6 Now place a ball of clay firmly on to the centre of the turntable and pat it firmly into a round shape.

7 Wet both hands and sprinkle a little water over the clay ball.

8 Check your stance — this is VERY important. Lean down over the

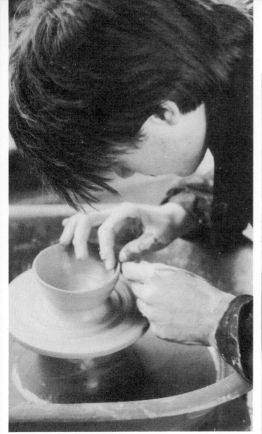

Thinning the rim of a pot — note position of arms and hands — they are controlled and rest on the bowl rim, this providing a levering action

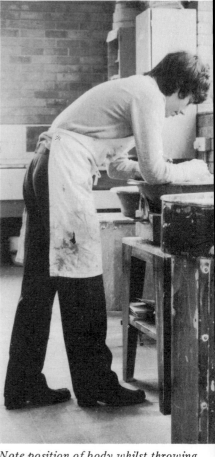

Note position of body whilst throwing a pot on a potter's wheel

Ball and cone action

wheel with your full weight being taken by your forearms, which should rest on the rim of the wheel-tray. Your nose should be directly above the centre of the turntable and the clay ball. By maintaining this stance you should not lose control and it should be easy to use your hands in a levering action.

9 Switch the wheel on to FULL speed and with hands firmly around the clay draw it up into a cone shape, then with one hand on top of the other press it down again into a ball shape. Repeat this action several times. This technique is called the ball and cone action and will assist with the centring of the clay and also condition it.

10 Ensure that the clay and hands are kept wet from now on, for if the clay dries it will stick to the hands and pull the pot off the wheel.

11 When the clay has been centred, with the back edges of the hands resting on the revolving turntable, drop the right-hand thumb into the centre of the clay and draw it gently outwards, steadying the clay with the left palm. Smooth the base (inside) of the pot at this stage.

12 Slow the speed of the wheel down to around half of the original speed.

13 The actual 'throwing' process: for this, rest forearms on the rim of the tray and, keeping both hands touching (the left fingers inside the pot and the right on the outside), lift the side of the opened clay form gently upwards in a levering action. When your fingers reach the rim of the pot, remove them GENTLY and SLOWLY. Often the knuckle of the right forefinger is used in this process — hence the term 'knuckling'.

14 Repeat this action several times, ensuring that the lifting movements are at roughly the same speed as that at which the turntable is rotating.

15 During this throwing process the pot should be shaped by exerting gentle pressure from the inside or on the outside of the pot.

16 It is important to remember that as you are constantly wetting the surface of the clay with a sponge, so the excess water that accumulates inside the pot must be removed, also using the sponge. If it is a tall pot it is advisable to use a dottle or a sponge tied to the end of a stick. Whilst throwing, do not allow your hands or the clay to dry but at the same time keep them, the pot and wheelhead as clean as possible — a muddy mess is confusing.

17 Should the rim of the pot become uneven (this is usually due to the clay moving out of centre at some stage) then hold a pin or sharp needle firmly to the outside of the rim whilst gently pressing the forefinger of your left hand on the inside. Do this whilst the pot is rotating and the uneven piece of clay can easily be removed and you will be left with an even rim. At this stage it may be necessary to clean the base of the pot and bevel it with a scraper or sharp tool.

18 For final smoothing, hold the sponge or turning tool gently against the pot whilst it revolves.

19 To remove the pot, stop the wheel, splash the turntable with plenty of water and pull the wire or fishing line gently between the pot and turntable. With DRY fingers move the pot gently to the edge of the

Cutting a pot off the wheelhead

turntable by its base, slide it off the turntable on to the palm of your hand and gently place it on a board to dry, using a tilting action. Never try to slide the pot directly from the turntable on to a board, as many a catastrophe has occurred in this way! A little practice will make perfect so do persevere.

20 Pots should be allowed to dry slowly (preferably in a damp cupboard or under polythene) and when 'leather hard' should be inverted, allowing the base to dry. Alternatively the pot should (at the leather-hard stage) be placed centrally on the wheelhead of the potter's wheel in preparation for a foot to be turned or reshaping to be carried out. In order to stick the rim of the pot firmly to the turntable, lightly moisten the rim and the turntable and press down gently, so causing a seal fo form. If this method is not satisfactory, three or four small knobs of soft clay may be pressed down on to the turntable against the pot — these will secure the pot whilst it is being turned. To turn the pot, hold a sharp turning tool firmly in both hands and support both elbows into your body or forearms on the rim of

Turned base of a thrown pot

Pot on a wheel — table model

the wheel. The technique of turning becomes a very personal one but with practice can be extremely fascinating. Remember that the wheelhead *must* always turn SLOWLY during the turning process and a lot of practice is required before success is obtained. It is a good idea to throw small pots especially for the purpose of practising turning.

TIPS

Distortion: when removing a pot with a wide rim from the wheel it is a useful tip to place a sheet of wet newspaper over the whole rim of the pot before cutting it off the turntable. This will prevent the shape of the pot distorting as it is removed — and as it dries.

Stacking: When biscuit firing thrown pots of the same size it is advisable to stack them in the kiln rim to rim as this will prevent distortion during the firing process. For the same reason, if a pot has a lid, allow it to rest on or in the rim of the pot during the biscuit firing.

Wet newspaper placed on rim of pot before removing from wheelhead (prevents distortion)

THE POTTER'S WHEEL

Safety: Before using a potter's wheel do check that you do not have long, loose hair — tie it back and be safe — if caught up in the revolving turntable it could be very dangerous!

Overalls: Use a good covering overall or apron — the beginner using the wheel usually gets smothered with wet clay!

Nails: Long fingernails are a nuisance as they score the clay and damage pots. They can also be very painful if they get torn.

Balsa wood: Keep odd pieces of balsa wood as they are the best aid that I know for cleaning and drying the wheelhead — just scrape a piece of balsa wood across the surface of the wet turntable.

Hands: Be sure always to remove your hands from a revolving pot VERY SLOWLY — even a slight nudge can ruin it!

Air Bubbles: If an air bubble should appear in the wall of a pot that is being thrown, stop the wheel, prick it open with a needle and gently add soft clay to the hole. Carry on with the throwing process.

Speeds: It is important to remember that the wheelhead must rotate quickly when centring the clay and then be reduced to a SLOWER speed for the actual making and shaping of the pot. Remember, too, that your hands should be lifting the pot at approximately the same speed as that at which the wheel is rotating.

VARIATIONS

Agate Ware: This is very attractive pottery and is made by colouring several different pieces of clay (using stains or oxides, as explained in Chapter 9) and twisting them together in a spiral action. The mixed clays are lightly kneaded together and a pot is thrown on the wheel. When leather hard the pot will require to be scraped or turned in order that the various coloured clays may reveal their agate-type patterns. After biscuit firing this type of pottery only requires to be decorated with a clear transparent glaze.

Three-dimension tiles: Very attractive tile pictures can be made by throwing small shapes and cutting rings from pots and applying these with slip to damp clay tiles. This techniques can be particularly effective if coloured clays are used or even with just a grey clay on a red clay tile background.

Thrown bowls

PULLING HANDLES

If handles are to be added to pots — and apart from being useful they can be very decorative — they must ALWAYS be pulled in the correct fashion and NOT be formed by rolling out a piece of clay and 'sticking' it on to a pot. To pull a handle correctly, make a roll of clay about the size of a fat sausage (ensure it is smooth and plastic) and, keeping it wet, pull the clay gently downwards between the joints of your thumb and forefinger. If you hold the clay over a bowl of water you can dip the hand that is stroking the clay into the water at the end of the downstroke of each pulling action. When the handle is pulled to the required length and thickness, place it flat on a board to dry a little. When it is at the same state of dryness as the pot to which it is to be adhered, score the two surfaces to be joined and add a little slip before pressing into position. John Colbeck gives an excellent detailed description of this process in his revised edition of *The Technique of Pottery* by Dora Billington. The base of a handle is a good place to impress your mark of identification. Many professional potters make their own stamp for this purpose by carving their initials in reverse into a small sausage of clay and then biscuit firing it. This then becomes the stamp with which to mark and identify pots.

Care of used Clay Do not throw clay which has been used on the wheel into the recycling bin. It may be too soft for immediate re-use, but if put aside to harden a little, and then kneaded again, it will become ready for use. If it is put into a bin with other forms of recycled clay it will be mixed with clays of different consistencies and so be much more difficult to prepare for throwing again. Always keep your throwing clay in a separate bin and, if it becomes 'tired', allow it to rest for a week or so. After it has rested add a little new clay and re-knead it — it will become as good as new and be ready for immediate use.

Turned vase and jug — note pulled handle

Maintenance of Pottery Wheels Pottery wheels do not need a lot of maintenance, but it is still advisable to service them regularly or have them serviced about once a year by a qualified engineer (usually the maker). If doing your own servicing, check electrical connections and insulation, also be sure that a wheel is not placed close to a radiator, particularly if it has grease nipples. These will tend to dry out quickly, so in any case keep a grease gun handy and give them a 'shot' of grease two or three times a year. It is also wise to check the bearings and grease them too if necessary. If a wheel is cleaned and washed over well after use — *every time* — it should not get clogged up and very few problems are likely to occur.

First Pots When first attempting to make pots on the wheel do not try to be too ambitious — keep them small and raise them vertically — don't aim to make bowls in the first instance. It is most import to master the art of raising a vertical pot first! However, if you do have a series of disasters don't despair — if your thumb keeps going through the bottom of the pot, make a grooved rim on it with your fingers and remove from the turntable. When you have a collection of these bottomless pots, thread them on a rope and make a snake — as in the illustration. These are great fun and look very pretty if each section is glazed and decorated in different colours. Add eyes to the pot that is to form the head and make the tail long and thin.

Bowl — thrown and turned

First thrown pots, wired together to form a 'snake'

8 Pottery made by using a Combination of Techniques

There are many ways in which interesting pottery can be made using a variety of techniques. With experience the potter can explore these possibilities and create some very unusual art forms and exciting pottery.

I shall explain below some ideas that are quite widely used and also one or two less usual ones.

THUMB OR PINCH POTS

Nativity figures: Made by wrapping the clay around a cone for the body and clothing and then adding a pinch pot for the head.

Cartoon characters and animals: Made by using two or three pinch pots and adding soft clay that has been pushed through a coarse metal sieve to make hair.

Book-ends: Using two tiles to form an 'L' shape, add a small pinch pot as support and to hold a small plant or bulb.

Fruits: Various pottery fruits may be made using the pinch-pot method and adding small leaves made by rolling the leaves out into thin clay, cutting around them and adding them to the pot.

Note: Most of these pots look best by being decorated with oxides before biscuit firing and then being glazed with a white opaque glaze (e.g. Podmore's P. 2116).

Cone figures around a maypole

Pinch-pot cat and dog and brick-pot wishing well

Slab-made shoes with coiled laces

Pinch-pot dog in slab-built dog kennel

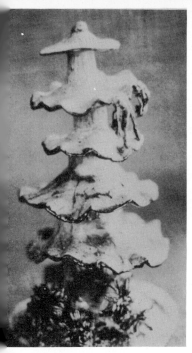 

inched fungus with sieved clay decoration   *Pinch pot with coiled neck and fold*

ROLLED CLAY AND WRAP POTS
Beer tankard: A tall wrap pot, if finished well, can make a good beer tankard if a stout handle is added. Alternatively a lip can be formed and the same shape will make a good jug.
Vase: A wrap pot with small clay leaves added on it makes a very attractive vase.
Leaf vase: Long leaves cut out in clay and wrapped around a cardboard former in an overlapping fashion make a very pretty leaf vase — or a bowl, if laid over a hump mould or in a dish mould.
A log posy pot: By making a wrap pot, scoring the surface to give a bark effect, making a hole in the side and laying it down lengthways a very attractive posy pot may be made — particularly if small leaves and little clay flowers are added for decoration.

BRICK AND COIL POTS
Thatched cottage: A brick pot made into a house with sieved clay added to the roof makes a very nice thatched cottage. These pots are usually best made using red clay for the bricks and grey clay for the 'thatch'. Before adding the sieved clay always score the surface thoroughly and add some slip. The sieved clay will often shed some of its pieces in its drying state and even at the biscuit stage, but all will be well once it is glazed and fired.
Wishing well: If making a 'wishing well' using bricks, 'thatch' can also be used, but even more interesting will be the addition of some pieces of broken blue glass, if you can obtain some, after the pot has been

dipped into the glaze and before it is glaze fired. If the pieces of glass are placed at the bottom of the well it will look as if there is water in the well! This idea particularly appeals to children.

Coil pot with handles: A coil pot — particularly a large one — looks very interesting if pulled handles are added — not necessarily functionally — for decorative purposes. Sometimes quite a few are added. Of course, handles may also be added to make jugs and casseroles, but for this the potter needs to be fairly skilled at his coiling.

Coil pot with thrown neck: A tall coil pot can sometimes look quite effective with a neck that has been thrown added to it.

MOULDED DISHES

Bottles: These may be made quite easily by making two moulded dishes (preferably oval) and joining them together. Cut a hole in one end and either coil a neck or add one that has been thrown. The base must be flattened so that it will stand up. These bottles often look well with a pulled handle added to each shoulder.

Bowls: A moulded bowl may have a foot turned on its base by adding a coil, inverting the bowl on to a potter's wheel and turning the foot so that it becomes part of the bowl.

Lids and tureens: These can easily be made by adding handles to moulded bowls — one each side for a tureen and one to the centre of the underside of a bowl which will then be inverted to form a lid.

A variety of techniques — coiled, slabbed, moulded, pinched and sculpted

Slab pot with coiled neck

Moulded bottles with coiled and thrown necks (note double glazing)

TILES AND SLAB POTTERY

Tiles: These can have all kinds of additions to give a three-dimensional effect. In the chapter on throwing I have already mentioned the idea of applying thrown pieces, but there are many other ideas such as clay leaf shapes, sieved clay, cut-out numbers and letters for door name and number plates and so on. These are particularly effective if oxides are used sensitively and then the tiles glazed with white opaque or transparent glazes. Mixtures of coloured clays are also very effective for such tiles.

Slab pots: These, of course, look very well if a shoulder is added and then a coiled or thrown neck made to compliment the pot.

POTTERY MADE BY USING A COMBINATION OF TECHNIQUES

The ideas I have given above are only a few that come to mind, and I am sure that every potter will come up with some of his or her own original ideas — this is half the fun of it — the more you explore the more exciting pottery becomes. Always be prepared to experiment with ideas — you will soon find out those that work and those that don't!

9 Decoration

There are many ways in which a pot may be decorated and tremendous satisfaction can be obtained by exploring some of the techniques so readily available to the potter who thinks and uses his imagination. However, the chosen form of decoration must suit the pot, it must have balance and enhance the pot. Although this aesthetic awareness comes with years of experience much can be gained by looking at and analysing the work of the craftsmen potters. There are many books containing beautiful photographs of such pottery and, of course, exhibitions to be visited where close-up studies may be made. Remember that as a picture frame should enhance a picture so the decoration of a pot should seem to belong to it and suit its shape. Owing to the fact that hand-built pottery — particularly by amateurs — is usually fairly robust it is inadvisable to aim for really delicate decoration unless working with a fine porcelain clay. For example fine writing and the painting of pictures do not generally turn out very successfully and this form of decoration is, therefore, best avoided. In this chapter I shall explain the methods of decoration that I have found to be most successful for general use.

TECHNIQUES AND IDEAS

Mixing colours: Some very interesting and unexpected patterns can be created by the use of two or three different coloured clays mixed together by kneading before making the pot. Coloured clays can be made by mixing oxides or body stains into slip (between 2% – 8% according to the strength of colour required) and then allowing the slip to dry to a plastic clay state. Colours can also be added to soft clay, but always knead well before use.

Pinch pot showing the combination of red (hat and eyes) and grey clays

DECORATION

Red and grey clays: If you have these two basic clays, some very interesting effects can be created by just using each clay individually whilst building a pot. For example, a house could be built with red brick walls and a grey roof and door. Remember, though, to glaze and fire such pottery to the temperature of the clay of the lowest optimum — this is usually in the earthenware temperature range — biscuit to 960°C (1760°F) and glaze fire to 1080°C (1976°F).

Coloured slips: These can be made up quite simply by adding the required amount of colour to white slip and sieving through an 80 mesh-sieve. The slip needs to be of a consistency equal to that of double cream. It can then be applied in a variety of ways as follows. (N.B. Slip must ALWAYS be applied to pottery whilst it is in its 'green' condition — i.e. never to clay harder than the leather-hard stage, or shrinkage problems will occur.)

Painting: It is wise to paint the outline on a pot first with powder paint or to use a stencil. Then paint the slip on the pot boldly, over the powder which will fire away leaving a clear slip outline. Impressions made in a clay surface often look well when painted with coloured slips. Any surplus or smudged slip may be scraped off leaving a clean finish.

Slip trailing: Before attempting this, decide on the pattern to be adopted and make a powder paint outline if necessary. Fill a slip trailer (be it an orthodox bulb-type slip trailer or a hairdresser's applicator bottle) with a thick coloured slip. Hold the nozzle of the trailer just above the surface of the clay and squeeze gently, drawing the nozzle firmly in the required direction. It is advisable to test the trail line on a piece of paper first in order to check the regularity of the flow.

Equipment for slip trailing

Slip trailing on a tile

Resist: This form of decoration can be done in several ways — using wax resist (for general use best purchased in solution form) which is painted on to the leather hard pot which, in turn, is then dipped into the coloured slip. This will not stick to the wax surface and consequently the pattern is left bare. Alternatively, pieces of dampened newspaper or wet leaves may be stuck to the pot and sponged over and dipped into the slip. Several hours later, when the slip has lost its shine and is therefore dry, the paper or leaves may be lifted off carefully with a pin. Several different coloured layers can be added in stages using this technique. However, it is important to ensure that each layer of slip is set before adding the next. After biscuit firing this type of decoration usually only requires to be glazed in a transparent glaze. N.B. Paper doilies make excellent resist patterns for tiles and plates.

Sgraffito: This Italian term means 'scratched'. It is an interesting form of decoration and consists of scratching away at a pot which has been dipped into a slip. The scratching reveals the colour of the clay underneath, but care must be taken as mistakes cannot easily be rectified. Sgraffito is particularly effective on tiles and here, again, a stencil can be very useful.

Marbling and feathering: Marbling is great fun; it is simple and can be successfully applied by even the inexperienced potter. For example, make a tile of clay and coat it with a coloured slip — pouring or dipping.

DECORATION

Next take a slip trailer containing another coloured slip and dot some slip on to the first coating whilst still wet. Swirl the tile around and a pretty marbled effect will be formed. This technique is very effective when applied to press-moulded or slip-moulded dishes and bowls, whilst still in the mould. For these use the same technique as for the tiles, coating the inside of the dish and pouring off the excess slip before applying the second colour and swirling around. Leave the dish and slip to dry before removing dish from its mould. For feathering, instead of dotting the second colour over the slip coating, trail several lines across the surface and then with a feather or a bristle draw lines through the slips in the opposite direction. This will cause drag marks which will form an attractive pattern. There are many variations on this theme and experimentation can be great fun.

Opaque glazes can be used over coloured slips but the effects tend to be muted — hence I recommend the transparent varieties.

Marbled and feathered slip-moulded dishes

Slip-decorated cat

Whilst still thinking of ideas to decorate pottery in its green state let us consider such methods as texturing, incising, inlay, applied and stamped ornamentation.

Texturing: Many interesting clay textures can be created from a wide variety of objects. Sometimes these objects can be pressed into or dragged over the finished pot, and sometimes it is better to texture the clay whilst in its initial plastic state, allowing it to dry slightly before carefully making it into its 'pot' shape — e.g. slab pots. Articles that could usefully be added to a box of texture aids might well include some of the following: — Bark, broken brick, rough string, polystyrene tile pieces, wire mesh, hair rollers, carved furniture casters, springs, buttons, corrugated paper rolled up, broken pieces of wood, odd stones, etc. And remember your own finger tips can often be your best tools — make imprints and try dragging them as they press into the soft clay, or pinch and twist. Also, collect a variety of different textured materials such as hessians, as these create effective textures when clay is rolled out over them.

Bottle textured by rolling clay over bark from a tree before making the pot

Tree pots with fungus — note texture

Contrasting textures of a 'flower'

Incising: Using a V-shaped lino-cutting tool, patterns can be incised into the surface of the pot and if the cuts are well pronounced these cuts will show up clearly and not disappear under a coating of glaze. Oxides can be effectively rubbed into the cuts and the surplus dusted off.

Inlay: Cuts made with a lino cutting tool can be filled with clay or slip of another colour. The surplus can easily be removed with a metal scraper. When adding plastic clay it sometimes helps to brush water or slip into the cuts to help the clay stick.

Fine texture of a simulated natural form

Incised pattern on a model

DECORATION

Applied and stamped ornamentation: Small pieces or strips of clay may be added in the form of a decoration to pots whilst still at the leather-hard stage. To do this the pot must be roughened where the pieces are to go and then the pieces or strips should be stuck on with slip. It is important that the piece of clay to be applied should be in the same soft state as the pot itself — if not, the added pieces will drop off as the pot dries.

Sprigging: This is another form of applied decoration and can be done by making a small mould of plaster of Paris and casting a suitable motif — it is a similar process to that used for large moulds. Alternatively, a motif can be carved into a piece of plaster; this can then be filled with slip or plastic clay can be pressed into it. Surplus clay should be cleaned off from the mould using a wooden or plastic spatula, the sprig removed gently from the mould and applied to the pot with slip. Should the clay sprigs tend to stick to the moulds, coat the plaster with a little soapy liquid or fine oil before use. Perhaps the best example of sprigging in modern times is to be seen on Wedgwood pottery.

Stamped ornamentation: This has been mentioned under the texturing paragraph when objects such as buttons, coins, keys, shells, etc. are pressed into the surface of a pot whilst it is still fairly damp. It is also useful to make small stamps of various shapes and designs and biscuit fire them. In the same way, as already mentioned, it is useful to make up a signet stamp (initials carved on in reverse) and when biscuit fired use it to stamp one's own pottery for easy identification.

OXIDES AND STAINS

Ceramic colours are known as metal oxides and pottery suppliers blend them to make very attractive stains. These oxides are finely ground to powder form so that they can be easily applied to clay when mixed with a liquid, usually water.

Underglaze colours: These are the oxides and stains and are best applied to clay *before* it is biscuit fired, The best form of application is the use of a fine brush — the best brushes of all are Japanese brushes with long bristles, but these are very expensive. Some professional craft potters do, in fact, paint their colours on to the biscuit fired ware but the disadvantage of this method is that when dipping the pot into the glaze some of the metallic particles will wash off into the glaze, smudging the decorative design and contaminating the glaze in the bucket. If the colours are applied to the clay before biscuit firing then the colours are baked into the clay and will not wash off. However, do be sure not to apply oxides and stains too thickly or they will create a barrier to the glaze. Never paint oxides as an all-over colour to a pot — it is much easier and cheaper to use a coloured glaze or slip!

In-glazing: This is an alternative form of applying colour to pottery and is the technique of applying oxides and stains over the unfired glaze, using a

84

very soft brush. The colours produced after firing will be much brighter using this method, but care must be taken not to damage the powdered surface of the glaze on the pot before it is fired. Particular care needs to be taken of the rims of pots, for if glaze is knocked off it will leave a bare patch on the finished pot. The most suitable base glaze for this technique is an earthenware white opaque or tin glaze.

Materials used
The colouring oxides and stains sold by pottery suppliers are as follows:
Metal Oxides: the most powerful form of colour – more powerful weight for weight than any other form of colour. Cobalt oxide (blue) is the most intense of all.
Metal carbonates: a less powerful form of colour.
Underglaze colours: these are fully intermixable to permit a very wide range of colour possibilities. These colours are much less intense than oxides and carbonates and, visually, look more like powder paints. If fired to recommend glaze temperatures they will retain their original colours.
Glaze and Body Stains: These can be added in quantities of 3% - 10% to glazes or 5% - 15% to slips and clay bodies. They can also be used as paints for direct application to an unfired glaze. These stains, too, are usually intermixable.
On-glaze colours: These are expensive and need to be applied with skill. They must be mixed with a liquid oil medium before applying to the fired glazed pot and then refired to temperatures varying between $730°C - 800°C$ ($1346°F - 1472°F$) according to the body used. They are usually applied using a brush or air-brush.

General Advice: All oxides, carbonates and underglaze colours can be mixed with water for application. They should be kept mixed in small quantities in screw-capped jars as they will not deteriorate with use provided CLEAN brushes are always used. Should they dry up, just add more water and mix – never throw away – these materials are much to expensive to buy in large quantities, so treat them with care. Manganese dioxide and the iron oxides are less expensive, but others, such as those containing cobalt or copper, are very highly priced. It is advisable to label the jars, as some of them are not easily distinguishable from one another in their soluble forms. When painting on to pottery, for best results paint thinly, ensuring that the colour in the container is kept *stirred* – if the particles are allowed to drop to the bottom of the jar you will find that only water from the top of the jar or much too thick a mixture of colour from the bottom is being applied. It is important to remember that powdered metal is very much heavier than water so will not stay in suspension for long. If it is painted on too thickly the resulting colour will be blackish and it will resist the glaze, leaving the coloured area starved of glaze. Try making test tiles using different thicknesses of colour and glazing them. You will be surprised at the results – for example, copper carbonate will vary from a pale green through to black.

DECORATION

Storage of metallic oxides and stains: It is advisable to store these colours in containers with good seals such as screw-top jars or plastic containers with firm clip-on lids. Do ensure that these containers are *labelled clearly* and *permanently*. It can be very difficult to recognize the difference between some oxldes — for example, manganese dioxide, copper oxide, cobalt oxide and nickel oxide, to the inexperienced eye, all look a similar shade of black. It is also wise to mark the maker and catalogue number as well, to fascilitate reordering.

Wax resist: The technique for using wax as a resist can be used with glaze decoration in exactly the same way as it is used with slips. It is also possible to mask parts of the pot so that these parts do not absorb the glaze. Some potters even apply wax to the bases of their pots so that they will be free of glaze during firing — this eliminates the process of wiping clean the bases of pots after dipping in the glaze.

DECORATIVE VARIATIONS

Glass: Coloured glasses mixed together or even on their own can give beautiful effects in the bottom of pots and dishes. Collect different coloured glass and store in a screw-top jar after crushing. The pieces of glass should just cover the bottom of the dish after it has been glazed and placed in the kiln for firing. The results can be quite fascinating. However, it is important that the dish rest absolutely HORIZONTAL in the kiln, or when the glass melts it will slop to one side and harden in that position as it cools. Mixing two colours can be very effective — e.g., blue and green or green and brown. Match the colours with the glaze that has been chosen to coat the pot. Wine bottles provide an excellent source for this purpose.

Burnishing: Burnishing is probably the simplest form of decoration and is particularly effective with red clay. It is best done when the pot is just beyond the leather-hard stage. Select fairly strong pottery for this purpose and then gently rub the surface of the pot in a circular motion with the back of a spoon, a piece of smooth bone or even a stone. A polish will result which will remain after the biscuit firing. This technique is particularly effective on pottery that is to be fired in sawdust or clamp kilns, as mentioned earlier, in Chapter 2.

On-glaze decoration: This is effected by painting on to the fired glazed pottery on-glaze colours or enamels. These colours need to be mixed with a special oil medium which is obtainable, together with the colours, from pottery suppliers. Brushes and surplus paint can be cleaned by using turpentine or turps substitute. These colours, when applied to the pottery, are then fired to a temperature around $760°C$ ($1400°F$).

Tools: Special mention should be made of the tools used for decoration — particularly brushes. The type of brush used can be very crucial to the end product, for every brush will give a different stroke. It is important, there-fore, to take great care of these brushes and to see they are kept clean and supple. Signwriters' brushes are particularly good to use, though the Oriental brushes are probably the best, though expensive! Select brushes that will give a variety of strokes and use the brushes with a firm movement from the arm, keeping the wrist fairly rigid. Always ensure that tools are washed thoroughly after use so that colours do not get intermixed unintentionally. It is important to remember that it is difficult to remove colours once applied, and a good pot can easily be spoiled with too much haste.

DECORATIVE USES OF GLAZES

1 Using coloured transparent glazes, trickle or spray small quantities over pots glazed with white opaque glaze. Domestic plastic spray bottles are quite useful for this purpose. Green transparent glaze over white is very effective, as is blue over part green, over white.

2 Take a coloured opaque base glaze and spray over it coloured transparent glazes, or pour streaks down the sides of a glazed pot.

3 A pot or tile with depressions in it may be glazed with a coloured opaque glaze and scraped clean over the raised surfaces, leaving a thick deposit of glaze in the indentations. These indentations may be thickened with a brush full of glaze, and if fired around $1080°C - 1100°C$ ($1976°F - 2012°F$) a pretty jewel effect will be obtained.

4 Red clay is very suitable for glazing with a white opaque glaze and then further decorating with coloured transparent glazes. The coloured glazes may also be trailed on to the base glaze using a slip trailer on polythene shampoo-type bottle with a fine nozzle.

There are many more possibilities so do experiment!

Stoneware glazes

Blue/grey and tenmoku glazes: Glaze an incised pot or one with applied decoration with blue/grey glaze, then scrape off the raised surfaces and paint them with tenmoku glaze. The effect will be a superb turquoise and rich brown combination. Coiled pots with the outside of the coils left unsmoothed are very effective when decorated in this manner. A lighter brown effect will be created if the raised surfaces are scraped and left unglazed — i.e. without the addition of the tenmoku glaze.

Copper carbonate used with a white stoneware glaze: Paint a mixture of copper carbonate and water on to the rims or use as a wash on the side of a pot (e.g. a slab pot) before biscuit firing. Then glaze with a white stoneware glaze. This technique is very effective on shell and rock sculptures, and works very well if hollows are shaded with varying intensities of copper carbonate. Broken glass pieces placed into hollows will give an attractive 'water' effect.

Random pouring of a second glaze: This technique is particularly effective on clay sculptures and large pots. For example, after coating in a white glaze, pour a coloured glaze (slightly thinned with water) over the pot at random, causing a trickled effect. Blue-grey glaze and tenmoku work well

DECORATION

when used in this manner, and sometimes a good effect is obtained by inverting a pot, either by holding it upside down or by placing it over a bowl or two narrow sticks — if it is too heavy to hold easily. Another good combination is iron oxide (red) painted under an oatmeal glaze — e.g. a grass or fern pattern painted on to the side of a mug before or after glazing with oatmeal.

Banding: Glazes and oxides can be applied to pots by using the banding method. To do this, place a pot on a banding wheel (turntable) and hold a wide brush, dipped in an oxide or coloured glaze, against the pot and gently spin the banding wheel. Try not to double coat. Single strokes give the best results — don't go round and round with the brush.

Advice: Whenever possible it is desirable to have in mind the type of decoration intended before the pot is even commenced. People should always be encouraged to think ahead. Obviously from time to time one may have second thoughts, but generally the best pots are created by those potters who have thought through the whole process from the initial choice of clay and the design of the pot to the final stage of decoration and glazing. With more complicated pottery it is advisable to make a rough sketch of the intended pot with a few notes added as to the decoration and glazes envisaged — this will help to keep the pot 'on line'. So often a pot is started with one idea in mind and then ends up being something totally different in the final stages. It is so easy to 'let the pot take over', and it is a good exercise to set down what is intended and to achieve that intention finally.

Hairy running dog

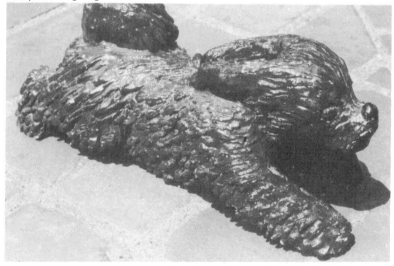

10 Glazes

Many books have been written on the intricacies and the chemistry of pottery glazes. However, in this chapter my aim is only to give brief guidelines that will enable potters to formulate a simple understanding of the practical application of glazes and so provide them with successfully glazed pottery.

Most people will ask the obvious question 'What is a glaze?' The answer is that glaze is a form of glass. Basically there is no difference between a glaze and glass except that glass is melted first and the shapes formed in the molten state, whereas a glaze is melted on a shaped clay surface, the biscuit-fired pot. Bernard Leach says of glazes: 'As clothes are to the human body so are glazes to pots'. They are made from a variety of clay-based powders and oxides and the end product, i.e. the colour, surface, texture and feel, will vary according the recipes used and indeed from batch to batch with the same recipe. I have heard glazes compared to wine inasmuch as, though they are basically quite simple, they do depend upon the subtle quality of their ingredients which may vary according to their source and age.

The purpose of a glaze is to make pottery non-porous and resistant to scratching and to create certain decorative effects. It should be useful *and* visually attractive.

Nowadays potters can purchase ready-made glazes, and in this way they reduce the complication of having to use many different firing temperatures and also save a lot of time and trouble obtaining and mixing a large variety of raw materials. However, there are a few stoneware glazes, particularly ash glazes, that are fun to mix and experiment with, and I will give a few recipes at the end of this chapter. It is generally considered wise to buy glazes from the same manufacturer you buy your clay from, because if the glaze is designed to go with the clay there will be no problems in making the glaze fit the ware and simple faults like crazing and peeling are less likely to occur.

Two types of glaze are normally used in studios — earthenware glazes which fire to around 1080°C (1976°F) and appear to lie on the surface of the pot, and stoneware glazes which fire to around 1260°C (2300°F) and actually fuse into the body of the pot. Reference is sometimes made to raw glazing — this is when glaze is applied to a green pot (at the leather-hard stage), dried and then fired to the temperature of the glaze. Ignoring

GLAZES

the biscuit stage can cause many problems and therefore raw glazing is not normally recommended — however, it can be fun to experiment with and some suppliers are now specializing in these glazes.

COLOURED GLAZES

A simple method of acquiring a variety of coloured glazes from base glaze is to add oxides to such glazes as transparent and white opaque earthenware glazes. Quantities vary from 1-5%. Combinations of oxides can be used, but experiment first with small quantities for they do not blend like paints and sometimes the results can be quite surprising.

It is a very good idea to keep a glaze recipe book showing the firing temperatures, times and recipes for each glaze. Record the results also and you will find that such a book will become invaluable over the years — particularly if you wish to repeat a particularly successful venture.

MIXING

All glazes are mixed in exactly the same way — that is, unless the manufacturer specifically suggests an alternative method, as sometimes occurs with crystalline glazes.

You will need: A two-gallon bucket and lid, a large mixing bowl or another bucket, a glaze mop (large brush), 80-mesh sieve, 120-mesh sieve, two slats 45 cm. (18 in.) long, bentonite, glaze powder, water, *and* a Kleenex type mask or a scarf tied around your nose and mouth.

If you do not have a glaze mop, tie a dozen large classroom-type paintbrushes together.

a Two-thirds fill the bucket with water — preferably warm water.

b Add to water about 4½ Kg. (10 lb.) glaze powder and 1%-2% by weight of bentonite (approx. 1 dessertspoonful) and mix in.

c Place the two slats over the bowl or second bucket and set the 80-mesh sieve on the slats.

d Pour the glaze and water mixture through the sieve, brushing in a circular motion all the time.

e Replace the slats over the original bucket and set the 120-mesh sieve on the slats.

f Pour the glaze, once sieved, through the 120 sieve, brushing in a circular motion once again.

g The glaze is now mixed, so LABEL BUCKET CLEARLY — e.g. White Opaque Glaze P. 2116 (E).

h Leave to stand for several hours — preferably until next day.

Tips

a ALWAYS label buckets and mark (S) for stoneware and (E) for earthenware. This indicates the temperature range the glazes are to be fired at.

b Always add bentonite, as this is a suspender and prevents the glaze sticking firmly to the bottom of the bucket when it has been left to settle.

c A rough guide for mixing a glaze is ½ Kg. (1 lb.) glaze powder to ½ litre (1 pint) of water.

90

Consistency of a glaze Before applying a glaze always check its consistency and adjust according to your requirements – i.e.:

a Assess the biscuit state of the pots to be glazed – i.e. if they have been fired to around 960°C (1760°F) a normal 'single cream' consistency will be required. However, if the pots have been underfired the glaze will need to be thinner than normal, as the pottery will be more porous. Conversely, should the pots have been overfired at the bisucit stage (i.e. over 1000°C) (1832°F), the glaze will need to be thicker than normal as the clay will have begun to vitrify. It always helps in such cases to heat the pots in the kiln to around 200°C (392°F) before applying the glaze, as the heating-up process will open up the pores and therefore make the pots more porous and the glaze easier to apply.

Glazed pot

b Test the glaze by pouring off about a pint of the still water resting on the top of the glaze in the bucket into a jar or bowl. Then stir the glaze well. Normally it will be fairly thick at this stage, but dip a DRY finger into the glaze and see how it coats your finger. It should have a smooth coating similar to that of single cream. If it is thicker than is required, put some of the original water back into the glaze bucket, testing as you do it — but do remember - ALWAYS use a dry finger! Bearing in mind the variations (according to the biscuit temperatures of the pots) proceed as follows — that is, when you have established that the glaze you are to use is of the correct consistency.

Tip: Before applying the glaze, check that the pots are not dusty. It is a good idea to sponge pottery over with a slightly damp sponge before glazing — this will prevent the dust particles resting on the surface of the pottery and so causing pinholes and tiny bubbles which will inhibit the smooth overall glazing process of the pottery.

Unglazed pot

APPLICATION

There are several methods of applying glaze to biscuit-fired pottery and I list some of them below:

Dipping and pouring: If the inside of a pot needs glazing, do this first by pouring some glaze from a jug into the pot, filling it to the brim and turning it as you pour it out again. Then hold the pot by its base and dip it into the bucket, holding it there for approximately 4-5 seconds. Remove slowly and hold still for a few seconds in the inverted position so that the drips will fall down into the bucket and not down the side of the pot. Then place the pot on a piece of newspaper. When dry (and this only takes a few seconds) clean off any glaze that has splashed on to the bottom of the pot, using a wet sponge — hold the pot upright as you do this to prevent any water trickling down over the fresh glaze on the pot. The glazed pot may be handled provided your fingers are dry and you use a

Glazing a dish by dipping – moving it in a semi-circular motion through the glaze

firm grip, taking care not to rub off the fresh glaze. If glaze is rubbed off at this stage it will leave a bare patch when fired, so particular care needs to be taken of rims and handles or any place on a model or pot that has sharp edges.

Slab pots made with grogged clay and a single glaze trickled over. The dish is carved and painted over the glaze (in-glazing)

Pouring (only): This method is used usually for awkward shaped models or sculptural forms, or when there is only a small quantity of glaze available. Proceed in the same way as explained in the paragraph above on dipping and pouring. However, instead of dipping the pot into the bucket, either hold the pot in one hand and pour glaze on to it from a jug held in the other hand whilst rotating the pot, or place the pot on two slats over the bucket and pour the glaze over it, catching the surplus glaze in the bucket beneath.

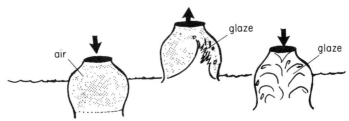

The action of dipping into a glaze

Brushing: Glaze can be applied with a brush, but this is not really recommended for general use as the effects can be patchy and streaky. It is, however, a very useful technique for touching up models with odd crevices that miss the pouring or dipping methods, or for touching up a bare spot that has been covered by the finger tips.

A second glaze: Double dipping, pouring or brushing a second glaze of a different colour over the first glaze can be very effective. A second glaze can also look well if splashed on. The important thing to remember is that the second glaze should be slightly thinner than that used for the first application. Stoneware glazes react particularly well with this technique.

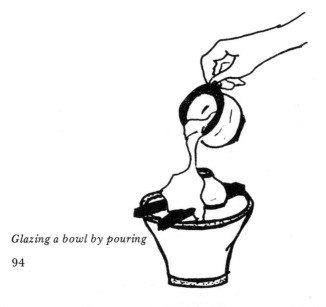

Glazing a bowl by pouring

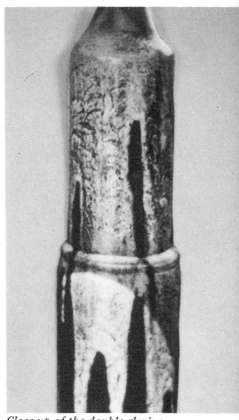

Lamp base — double glazed   *Close up of the double glazing*

FIRING

As soon as the glaze is dry the pots may be packed into the kiln and fired. When doing this do ensure that no two pots touch each other and check that *all* the bases of the pots are free from glaze. At high temperature glaze becomes molten and sticky and so pots that touch will stick together on cooling. A good method for checking that pots do not touch is to place the first pot in the kiln, then move the next up to it until you feel it touch, then move it away a fraction. In this way valuable kiln space is not wasted and you can be certain that the pots are not touching. It is necessary always to check the firing temperature recommended by a manufacturer of a glaze and it is best not to mix glazes of different firing temperatures if accurate results are expected. Never open the kiln door until the kiln is cold. It is extremely tempting to have a peep in the latter stages of the cooling process but if a draught is introduced into the kiln crazing will sometimes occur, which is a great pity after all the weeks of hard work and waiting!

GLAZES

Tips

a An important point to remember is that the glaze in the bucket should be kept constantly stirred, as glaze particles are heavier than water and will tend to drop to the bottom of the bucket. Very often 'starved' pottery is due to this omission. The glaze mixture in the bucket may be perfect but it has not been kept stirred and so the vital particles of glaze needed to complete the process have never reached the pot. It is necessary to understand that when a glaze is mixed with water it does not dissolve, it is only in suspension.

b Remember that if a large quantity of pottery is to be glazed at one time it will be necessary to check the consistency of the glaze periodically and sometimes extra water may need to be added. The reason for this is that porous pottery removes more water than glaze particles, with the result that the glaze in the bucket will become thicker as more pots are glazed. When a piece of pottery is dipped into a glaze the water is absorbed into the biscuit-fired clay leaving a coating of glaze on the outside and this, when fired, creates the glaze (or glass) layer. The water in the glaze bucket is only there to facilitate the application of the powdered glaze to the pottery.

c Should a pot become really messy during the glazing process — for example, if it is inadvertently dropped into the bucket or too much glaze is poured on to it — it can be washed off. Endeavour to collect the washed-off glaze, as it can be returned to the bucket. When the pot is clean again it should then be refired to biscuit temperature before reglazing. If in a hurry it is sometimes possible to just reheat the pot and glaze it whilst it is hot. Glaze sticks much more readily to a hot pot than to a cold one.

d Generally leave a rim of approximately 5mm. (¼ in.) clear of glaze at the base of a pot — this will allow for any glaze that might run down or even 'stretch'.

e In the event of an uneven powdered glaze surface, this may be gently rubbed off or scraped off with a razor blade before firing. However, do be sure not to create bare patches.

f When attempting to reglaze over a pre-fired glaze, ensure the glaze to be applied is really thick (at least double cream consistency) and always warm the pot before glazing.

g When a bucket of mixed glaze has been left for a long time the water may have evaporated. In such a case do not throw the solid mass away, as it can easily be reconstituted. Just break up the mass at the bottom of the bucket, add fresh water and sieve. It will be ready for use again in the same way as a newly mixed glaze.

Ordering glazes: It can often be very confusing and difficult to know where to start when faced, for the first time, by an array of pottery catalogues and the task of 'ordering some glazes'. For those in such a predicament I give below a few suggestions that will assist in the choice of a few base glazes. The earthenware glazes are particularly suitable for potters with small kilns, as these fire at a temperature of around 1060°C - 1080°C (1940°F - 1976°F). The stoneware range of glazes really require a more robust kiln as the high temperatures at which they must fire (around 1260°C, 2300°F) will soon cause a small kiln to wear out — even if it *will* reach this temperature, which is usually a bit of a struggle! Therefore check that your kiln is able to reach stoneware temperatures before buying such glazes. Most kilns over a capacity of two cubic feet have no problems in this way.

Earthenware glazes

Transparent glaze: this is not an expensive glaze and is very useful to use purely as a transparent glass covering for pottery or for mixing with colours to form coloured transparent glazes. I would suggest 2½ Kg. (5 lb.) of a glaze similar to Podmore's P. 2106 initially.

White opaque glaze: A vellum-type opaque glaze is pearly smooth to the touch and is one of the most useful glazes of all. Colours may be added to it and it also blends well with a coloured transparent glaze which can be applied over it. My preference in this range of glazes is Podmore's P. 2116 — again, 2½ Kg. (5 lb.) should be ample to start with.

Honey glaze: This is a lovely glaze producing a deep rich colour over red clay and a light golden colour over grey clay. Podmore's P. 2140 is ideal, but do keep it stirred as it is used and apply the glaze fairly thickly.

Stoneware glazes: There is an extremely wide choice of glazes in this category so it tends to become a matter for personal choice. It is best to start off with about four basic glazes which will fire to temperatures of around 1260°C - 1280°C (2300°F - 2336°F).

N.B. If glazes should become contaminated by colours do not throw away but keep as a base glaze and add a darker colorant. In this way an extra glaze will be added to your stock. These mixed-up remnants of glazes are often ideal for sculptural models.

11 Faults and Remedies

Unfortunately no matter how carefully pottery is planned and made, from time to time faults are bound to occur which may cause breakages, glaze imperfections and even ruined pots. This can be a heartbreak situation but if it is possible to analyse the cause then a repetition is unlikely to occur. It is when a fault recurs frequently that problems really begin.

In this chapter I intend to take a look at some of the most common faults and consider their causes. Even the occasional fault can be extremely vexing and particularly so if there is no obvious solution.

REPAIRING BREAKAGES
Greenware: Should a piece of pottery break before it has been fired it may be difficult to mend unless the clay is heavily grogged. Grogged clays, such as crank or sculpting marl, can usually be rejoined with light sponging and a little slip. However, if a piece of a pot made from a smooth clay breaks off it is much more difficult to mend. In such cases the pot and pieces must be gently sponged over, wrapped in a damp cloth and placed in a sealed airtight polythene bag for a couple of days. When the pieces have returned to a damp condition they can then be joined together again using slip. It is important that the pot be allowed to dry slowly. If speed is essential dry pieces of unfired clay can sometimes be joined successfully by using vinegar, lightly brushed over the broken edges, instead of water or slip. The vinegar reacts with the surface clay causing it to form a sticky slip which will aid the joining of the broken pieces. It is an interesting chemical process and the technique is worth experimenting with.
Biscuitware: When biscuit-fired pottery breaks it is usually not worth keeping unless it is possible to glaze the pieces separately and join them, after firing. with Araldite or a similar strong glue. Occasionally it is possible to balance the glazed piece or pieces on the glazed pot and fire it. Then, hopefully, the glaze will fuse the pieces together and so act as the 'glue'. Unfortunately these methods usually leave a hairline crack, so are not always satisfactory.

CAUSES OF FAULTS DURING BISCUIT FIRING
Breakages: If a pot breaks or blows up in the biscuit-fired kiln it is often due to the fact that the pot or parts of the pot have been made solid or too thick. Walls of uneven thickness may also cause problems due to uneven shrinkage during firing. Another common cause of a pot blowing

up is when it has been packed into the biscuit kiln before it is *really* dry. Handles and added parts to pots will often fall off a pot during firing if they were not in the same state of dampness when joined. Remember that a pot that varies considerably in its thickness or one which has dried too rapidly will undergo uneven contractions of the clay and will invariably crack or break during biscuit firing. One possible way of solving the problem of firing these pots is to ensure that they are absolutely dry and that the temperature of the biscuit kiln is raised very, very slowly.

Mending cracks: Cracks that appear in the biscuit firing of the pot are usually caused by poor joining of seams in the initial making. They can be filled with a special filler or 'stopping' that can be purchased from pottery suppliers. To do this, wet the crack to be filled and fill with a stiff mixture of stopping (usually mixed with water). Then refire the pot to biscuit temperature before glazing 'Pyruma' – the household fire cement – can also be used quite satisfactorily for this purpose.

Air bubbles: If the biscuit-fired pottery has bulges in it, it is usually due to air trapped in the clay before firing. This is caused by insufficient wedging and kneading and, possibly, failure to prick out air bubbles in the plastic clay mass, when making the pot.

Plaster of Paris: Small grains of plaster, if they become contaminated with the plastic clay, cause many problems at later stages. In the bisucit-fired ware pieces of pottery will blow or crack off, leaving a hole or broken face edge – it is usually possible to see the speck of plaster at the base of the hole. Occasionally a small speck of plaster will survive the biscuit-fired stage but will cause part of the glaze-fired pot to erupt – maybe several weeks after it has been removed from the kilns! The only remedy is to ensure that plaster of Paris never comes into contact with plastic clay – ALWAYS throw away any clay that has become contaminated or keep it well apart in a clearly labelled bin, to be used only for mould making. Of course, it is best not to use plaster of Paris at all in a clay area, then unfortunate accidents cannot occur.

Underglaze colours and oxides
Blistering: This is usually caused by the colours being applied too thickly. Sometimes the effect will be to create a black metallic surface that is devoid of colour and will not absorb glaze.

PROBLEMS WITH GLAZE FIRING
These can be many and varied but a few of the most common are:
Crazing or cracking: Usually due to the fact that the glaze has been applied too thickly or the pottery has been cooled too quickly after firing, often caused by the kiln door being opened too soon. A mismatched glaze can occasionally cause this problem – i.e., the glaze does not match the clay body used and the glaze may shrink more rapidly than the clay, causing this effect. The simple answer is to buy clays and glazes from the same supplier. However, this problem does not often occur with educational materials, fortunately.

Crawling: This is when the glaze crawls away in patches from some areas of the pot, leaving them bare. The cause is often dust or grease on the pot and, sometimes, too thick a layer of glaze being applied to the pot. This fault can sometimes be remedied by heating the pot to around 200°C (392°F), reglazing the bare patches and refiring. Personally, I do not find this a very satisfactory solution — take better care next time!

Blistering: Usually due to a glaze or one which has the wrong balance of ingredients. If the glaze used is a 'home-made' one, check the weight ratio next time.

Runny and bubbling glaze: If the glaze runs down the pot or has a rather unpleasant molten look about it, the cause is usually overfiring. Sometimes the cause can be in the glaze itself and then the addition of a little china clay or flint may help. Occasionally this bubbling effect can be due to underfiring when the surface of the pot is still dry.

Peeling or flaking: This is the opposite of crawling and is due to the body shrinking more than the glaze.

Starved glaze: This is caused by the glaze being too thin when applied to the pot. It may be that there is too much water mixed in with the glaze or quite simply that the glaze in the bucket is not kept stirred — hence more water than glaze is applied.

Stuck ware: When pots in a glaze-fired kiln have been allowed to touch they will invariably stick together. The only remedy is to attempt to break them apart and then to file or grind the sharp edges where they have been joined. In the case of stuck shelves — i.e. when pottery has stuck to the shelves due to a runny glaze — the only solution is to try soaking shelf and pottery in hot water for an hour or so — they will generally part company fairly easily, and only a little cleaning up (grinding or filing) will be necessary. To prevent this happening again, ensure the shelves are coated with bat wash and silica sand and check the quality of the glazes used. Also check the firing temperatures used for the respective glazes.

Colours firing away: This is mostly due to overfiring, which causes the colours to decompose. Of course, it can be due to colours being applied *too* thinly.

Bloated pottery: This occurs when a pot is overfired at the glaze-firing stage, causing the clay body not only to vitrify but to begin to melt — so that bubbles form.

Warped pottery: This is due to unevenness in the making and in the walls of the pottery — or to overfiring.

Powdery glass: When using pieces of broken glass to decorate pottery in the glazing process, it is advisable to fire to as high a temperature as possible. Sometimes a white film or blobs of a soda-type substance tend to form on the surface of the glass when it has been fired to only earthenware temperatures, even though the glass has melted properly. This white powder can be wiped off with a damp cloth and will disappear completely after a few weeks. However, glass fired to stoneware temperatures will not often have this problem.

Adjustment of glaze consistencies: Should a biscuit-fired pot be overfired, causing problems with the glaze adhering and being absorbed by the pot, reheat the pot before attempting to glaze it and whilst it is still hot glaze it with a slightly thicker glaze. Conversely, if the pot is underfired, do *not* heat the pot but thin the glaze by adding more water, as in this state the pottery will be more absorbent than usual.

Filling cracks in white glazed pottery: A mixture of 'Araldite' and zinc oxide makes a very satisfactory filler and requires no further firing.

SLIPS

Although the application of slip is a simple process it is easy to make mistakes if certain rules are not obeyed. The most common problems are:

Peeling slip: This is due, usually, to the pot being too dry when dipped into the slip or when the slip is applied to it. The two bodies shrink at different rates which causes the peeling.

Distortion: This sometimes happens to bowls and dishes when made in mould and then coated with slips. Provided the bowls are allowed to dry to a leather-hard stage in a mould (or, if this is not possible, are supported by rolls of clay) and then when removed from the mould inverted on to a board to dry, distortion should be minimized.

Lumpy surface: This unpleasant effect is caused when the slip has not been sieved (80 mesh) prior to use. Unlike glazes, slips need to be re-sieved if left more than a day or so. It does not take many minutes to sieve a slip and the perfect results are worth the effort.

101

12 Further Ideas

In this chapter I shall give a few further recipes for simple pieces of pottery, such as any 'hobby potter' may find it possible to make.

Night-light holder: Using a tile cutter or card template, make six tiles of the same size. Make holes of different shapes in the faces to form a pattern and make a hole large enough in the top face of the cube so that a wax night-light may be put inside the cube. As explained earlier in the slab-making section (chapter 4), the sizes of the tiles will have to be calculated, taking into account their thickness, before attempting to build the cube which is to contain the night-light. If it is to hang, remember to pierce two small holes in the top so that a cord may be threaded through by which to hang it.

Elephant and duck made using the pinch-pot method

Letter or toast-rack: This, also, is made using the slab technique. Use small boards to support the sections as they dry in a vertical position. A very attractive idea is to make these racks out of letters – e.g. T O A S T each letter being a section of the rack.

Animal collection: e.g. ducks, mice, hedgehogs, fish, owls, turtles, elephants, made from thumb pots and snakes, Loch Ness monsters made from coils.

Owl pots: These make most attractive storage pots and can be made in a variety of ways:

a A thrown pot with a second smaller thrown pot made to fit on the larger bottom one. The smaller pot which is the lid should be fashioned to the shape of an owl's head by carving into it and adding pieces for its beak, etc. With a tool such as a lollipop stick make feather patterns

Butterfly letter rack.

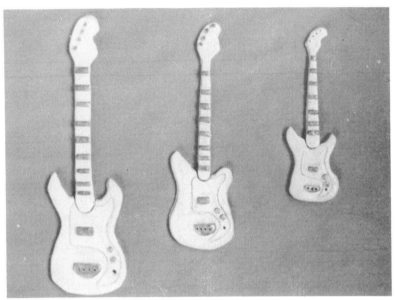

Guitar tile panel

all over the two pots. Decorate with iron and manganese oxides and glaze with a transparent or opaque glaze. This type of pot can look extremely effective if made from red clay and either left unglazed on the outside (just glaze the inside with a transparent glaze to make it waterproof) or glazed in a honey glaze.

b These owl pots may also be made using the coil technique or, with a little adaption, the wrap method. Experiment and, of course, study owls or pictures of them to get the correct expressions.

Shell ashtrays: These can be made by rolling out a slab of clay and turning up the edges in a wavy-edged effect to create the shape of a shell. Support the raised edges with rolls of clay until they become firm, and try to keep the base of the dish flat so that when it has been biscuit fired and then

103

Owl and squirrel pinch pots

glazed, the base may be sprinkled with pieces of broken blue and green glass. The glass will fuse together during the glaze firing and give the impression of water in the bottom of the shell-shaped dish. As mentioned earlier on, it is better to fire pots with glass in them to a stoneware temperature in order to avoid the soda effect (white dusty specks) which often speckle the fired glass for a time when only fired to an earthenware temperature.

Profiles: These are simply tiles which have been cut out to a shape that will represent a chosen form which will stand up — such as:

An animal profile: e.g, two squirrel-shaped tiles which, when they have been cut out, are joined (hinged) at the back edge of the squirrel's bushy tail (see illustration). These profile shapes may, of course, represent any object at all, provided it is possible to hinge the two tiles at one point so that they may stand upright — as does a book when opened.

A raised profile: An alternative form of profile object may be made by cutting out one tile shape as the complete flattened form (think of a tiger rug) and then raise the centre part by resting it over a hump form. Very young children can make attractive animal shapes in this manner with only a little assistance. It is best to give them a card template to cut around to make the basic shape — the rest is then quite easy.

Zodiac tiles: These are quite easy to make provided you can make a tracing. First, find a picture of a sign of the zodiac that you wish to transfer to a tile and trace it carefully. Don't get too ambitious to begin with — keep the outline fairly simple. Next, roll out a piece of clay to the

Turtle profile

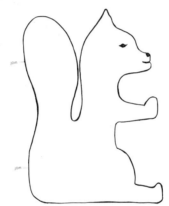

Squirrel profile, using two tiles

Animal profile — squirrel

105

thickness you require your tile to be and make grooves in the back of it to prevent it curling as it dries. Smooth the edges carefully and then place the tracing on the slab. With a needle, prick holes at close intervals all along the tracing through to the clay beneath — like a tattoo. Remove the tracing and gently inscribe the pattern more fully with a thicker needle or pointed tool. The sign of the zodiac will now have been transferred to the tile and may either be painted with oxides and stains between the lines or the lines themselves painted with a very fine brush. After biscuit firing, glaze with a transparent or opaque earthenware glaze. These tiles make lovely presents — particularly for birthdays — and look very well hung up as a wall plaque or made into teapot stands. Of course, if you feel really ambitious make the whole set and fit them into a frame to make a table top.

Zodiac tile — Leo

Unglazed but burnished red tile 'leaves' mounted on hessian to form a picture

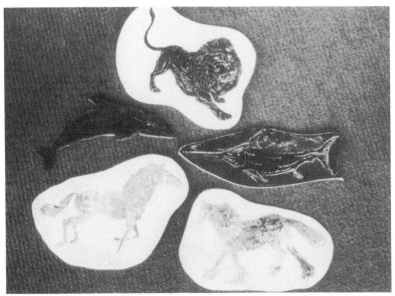

Zodiac and animal tiles

Tile pieces threaded into a macramé hanging

FURTHER IDEAS

Mosaic: This is work involving the arrangement of tiles of various colours and sizes, often very small ones. It is a useful way of using up odds and ends of clay, slips and glazes — however, ensure that all the tesserae (small tiles) made are of equal thickness. To make the tesserae, roll out a slab of clay, using strips of wood as a gauge for thickness. Cut it, using a needle, into small squares not more than 3 cm. (1 in.) square — sometimes it is effective to make them even smaller. Cut some of the squares diagonally so that you have some triangles. If the tesserae are to be coloured with slip this is best done before the slab is cut, pouring the slip over it. Alternatively, of course, the tesserae can be dipped individually but this is a much slower way of doing it — however, it is sometimes necessary if only a few of a particular colour are wanted. N.B. If doing a lot of mosaic work it could be worth while buying a tesserae cutter — this is like a very small tile cutter. Interesting work can also be created by using various coloured clay bodies. Even the simple contrast of red and grey clay can be most effective, and other colours can be made by making slip and adding oxides and stains to give colour — these slips when dried will produce coloured clay bodies. When the tesserae are quite dry they should be laid as flat as possible in the kiln and biscuit fired; they can then be dipped into a glaze. This process needs patience, as only the top face should be coated with glaze and it is important that when placed in the kiln the tesserae should not touch one another. The glaze, of course, can also be used as a method of colouring the tesserae and is a useful way of using up small quantities of coloured glaze.

Before starting to make the mosaic it is a good idea to put the tesserae into boxes, each containing a different colour. If the mosaic is intended for the top of a table or a picture it is sometimes easier to make it in a number of small sections — this particularly applies if the finished surface is to be large, as it might well be for a wall. If the tesserae are to be stuck to a board polyfiller is ideal, and it is also ideal for filling the gaps between them. Of course, there are other kinds of mosaic using pieces of different shapes to those mentioned above — hexagons, rectangles etc. Larger ones can be set in concrete and both concrete and plaster can be used to make decorative and textured backgrounds. Similar kinds of work can be done using shells, pebbles, broken glass and china — even pasta.

Calendars: Ceramic calendars make wonderful Christmas presents and are simple to make. The example illustrated is of an owl calendar but, of course, it can be of anything that suits the occasion. It is made by tracing the owl (or whatever) and transferring the drawing to a slab of clay and cutting around it to form the shape. The detail is pinpointed through the tracing as for the zodiac tiles. For calendars it is often better to paint the oxides and stains on top of the unfired glaze in order to obtain brighter colours. Don't forget to make two holes for the calendar to hang from and one or two for the wall-fixing string!

Face calendar built up from a variety of tile-shaped pieces

Owl calendar

FURTHER IDEAS

Necklaces: Apart from pendants there are many ways of making ceramic necklaces — from small patterned tile pieces threaded together to really hunky beads. To make beads it is best to roll the clay into small pellets, make a hole through each and flatten each side through which the hole is. The beads can then be glazed, after biscuit firing, and cleaned off on one side in order that they may be placed in the kiln without rolling around. As the hole is in the unglazed side the lack of glaze will not be noticed once the beads are strung together. Beads made from red clay and burnished are very effective, particularly if they are carved — these do not need to be glazed at all. Leather thonging is ideal for this type of necklace — it gives it a rather attractive primitive effect.

Parsley pot: A very popular form of kitchen pot which can be made by either coiling or throwing on a wheel. The only additions to the conventional pot are that holes are cut in the sides of the pot at selected places (about eight in all) and these holes are pulled out to form a lip so that the parsley or herbs may grown through these apertures. Pots of this type can be fairly heavy and may be glazed or made using red clay and left unglazed. Remember if unglazed they will need to be kept outside, as they will be porous!

Wall plant holder: These are most useful and very decorative and do not need to be glazed. A simple one can be made by making a flat tile for the back and adding half a mould dish for the front part of the pot. Scuff and join the seams thoroughly using slip, and carve or press a pattern into the clay to make it decorative. If it is not to be glazed, copper oxide or carbonate is effective if rubbed into any indentations or grooves. Remember to make a hole for screwing it to the wall.

SUMMARY OF USEFUL TIPS

Turntables: (i.e. banding wheels) If you are contemplating the purchase of one of these and feel rather nervous about the price, look around until you can find an old gramophone at a jumble sale or junk shop. Remove the turntable and mount it on a wooden plinth so that it may spin freely. Cut off the protruding spindle (that holds the records in position) with a hacksaw — this is so that you do not have a hole in the base of every pot you place on the banding wheel!

Recipe book and log book: I recommend all potters to keep a log book and a recipe book right from the very beginning, as it is amazing how often one wishes one could remember just what process was involved in the creation of a particularly successful pot. Write down all recipes and odd tips that you learn, and always keep a log of firings: the time the kiln was switched on, and switched from low to high, and when it was switched off; the temperature the kiln was fired at, the date and a rough list of what was fired in the kiln on each occasion. Also keep a record of what glazes and oxides you use and in what combinations, and comment on the final results — fantastic or horrible!

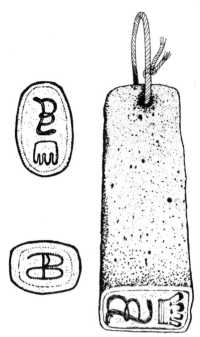

Potter's stamp

Coiling: Keep coils slightly shorter than you think you want, to prevent sagging. Make two or three pots at the same time so that one can be left to harden off whilst working on the next.

Vinegar: Can assist in the mending of broken greenware.

Signet stamp: Make a stamp with your initials carved into it in reverse and biscuit fire it. Use it for impressing your personal sign on to your pottery. The letters on a banker's card or credit card can be useful for this purpose.

Shrinkage: Remember in your calculations that shrinkage is approximately 8% − 10% from the initial making stage to the finished pot − make allowances for this.

Plaster slabs: Make one or two large enough for kneading your wet clay on and also for use in the drying out of recycled clay − a lot of money can be saved in this way, as no clay is wasted.

Balsa wood: Remember how useful a small piece of balsa wood is when used to clean and dry a wet wheelhead during throwing.

Glass: ALWAYS wrap up well any glass that is to be broken into small pieces and, as an extra precaution, wear glasses or sunglasses, just in case a small piece of glass should escape and fly loose. Keep different coloured pieces of glass in different labelled jars − with lids.

111

FURTHER IDEAS

Once-fired glazes: These are now more readily available than in the past, but it is always best to head the manufacturer's advice on how this type of glaze is to be applied, as the mode of application can vary with different types of once-fired glazes. Sneyd Ceramics of Stoke-on-Trent are amongst the foremost suppliers of this type of glaze. Once-fired pottery is not as durable as normal twice-fired pottery but it is less expensive to produce owing to the elimination of one firing. Try it!

Newspaper: Wrap it around tubes, tins, jars, etc., when making wrap pots. It will prevent the clay sticking to the core, which will then be easy to remove.

Turning tools: Simple turning tools can be made by bending short lengths of packing-case steel bonding strips. Bend a piece into a 'U' shape and pin to a wooden handle. They retain their sharp edges and can be made into various shapes, as required.

Packing a kiln: When packing a glaze firing remember always to place your pot inside the kiln, push it gently up to the next pot so that it *just* touches and then withdraw it a fraction. The pots will not then stick together, large gaps in the kiln between pots will be eliminated and space will be saved.

Bottoms of pots: Unless using stilts (which I do not generally recommend because of the sharp points that are left behind) *always* wipe the bottom of pots clean with a sponge before placing in the glaze kiln. Clean a slight rim (about 1 cm. ($\frac{3}{8}$in.) deep) of glaze around the bottom of the pot if it is to be stoneware fired.

Cones: When placing a cone in a kiln, in order to ensure the cone is in a visible position, place a torch inside the kiln and shut the door. If suitably placed the cone will then be visible through the spy hole. However, remember to remove the torch before firing!

Overfired and underfired pottery: If the biscuit-fired pottery has been either overfired (too high a temperature) or underfired (too low a temperature) it will be necessary to adjust the consistency of the glaze to be used. It will need to be thicker for an overfired pot and thinner for an underfired pot. If a pot is hot it will absorb more glaze than will a cold one, so bear this factor in mind when glazing an overfired biscuit pot, it sometimes pays to warm it up.

TEN TIPS TO HEALTHY POTTING

1. Clean potters are healthy potters — don't eat or drink or smoke in the workshop.
2. Wash your hands and face before leaving the working area or immediately after leaving.
3. Clean up immediately when spillages occur, using sponge and water — don't leave it until tomorrow, when it will have to be scraped up and so cause dust.

4 Keep benches, floors, walls and windows clean.

5 Always clean with water — don't brush!

6 Remember dust can be dangerous to your lungs, so don't make any! Use a mask when sieving or mixing dry ingredients. If sanding dry clay, do so over a bowl of water.

7 Wash protective clothing regularly and, for preference, use nylon or terylene overalls that do not harbour dust.

8 Ingredients are best kept in plastic or glass containers, but if this is not possible and a package is damaged, rebag and relabel it at once. Ensure that all pottery materials are labelled — preferably with name AND supplier's catalogue code number.

9 Regarding machinery and kilns, remember wiring is a job for experts only. Never remove guards from machinery such as pug mills. Ensure that no water gets on to motors or switches. Keep all equipment regularly serviced.

10 Keep a lidded dustbin handy for disposal of used packages and rubbish, and empty it regularly.

13 Making it Pay

As this chapter is about how to make your hobby pay, I shall suggest a
few of the ways in which I have known hobby potters to cover their
costs quite adequately and even make a profit so that they can buy extra
equipment and materials, or even a larger kiln. However, I do feel it is
important to approach the whole matter quite gently, getting your ideas
known by talking to friends and neighbours about what you are doing
and what your intentions are. Don't expect to make a fortune overnight!

POTTERY PARTIES

The least commercial way of making some money is to have a pottery
party in the form of a coffee morning or evening where the pieces of
pottery that you have for sale are on display, and invite neighbours and
friends — rather in the style of a 'Tupperware' party. At these occasions
people will often ask you to make things for them to order. This provides
an opportunity of discussing their requirements and your abilities, in
more detail. Be careful not to overcharge for pieces of pottery (check
similar shop prices) but, on the other hand, don't put stupidly low prices
on your goods or you will find it difficult later to raise prices to a sensible
level.

CRAFT FAIRS

Many craft fairs are now being held around the country, and it is usually
quite easy to persuade someone with a different craft to share a stall with
you so that you may sell some of your pottery — obviously you will have
to pay your share of the cost of the stall but, without doubt, for just a
day's fun you will make a reasonable profit, particularly just before
Christmas and Easter.

MARKET STALL

This is a little more arduous. Usually you are required to take a stall for a
set period of time, so you will need quite a lot of pottery before attempting
this type of selling. However, here again, you may be lucky enough to find
someone who is willing to share a stall with you. The Sunday markets are
particularly lucrative — it is the time when people have time to stand and
stare. But watch them — they may hold and drop too!

SHOPS

In the past I have found it extremely good business to visit a few small craft shops in small towns and villages and suggest to them that they sell small quantities of pottery on a sale or return commission basis. In other words, you state the price you want for a piece and the shop will either mark up its own price and so obtain a profit or they will ask you to increase your asking price to include their commission – say 20%. Provided the pottery you supply has a general appeal very little is ever returned, and you will soon find out what items are the most popular as you will be asked to repeat them. In this way you will soon get the feel of what is required.

EXHIBITION AND SALE

I have known several potters who have held their own exhibition of work, in a local hall (scout hut, village hall, or arts centre). Items that are not for sale should be marked N.F.S. and catalogued as such. From this form of exhibition quite a lot of commission work arises – so be prepared to be busy over the months ahead!

SHARING A STUDIO OR WORKSHOP

If you have been able to set up a small studio and have equipped it well but find the costs rather high, it can sometimes be a good idea to allow a friend to come in and share your facilities and kiln space, for a fee. I think the charge should probably be so much per hour and a firing fee charged for the use of the kiln. (This has to be worked out proportionately in relation to the amount and size of the work to be fired.) Another way of charging is for materials, by weight of clay, to include use of glazes and oxides – e.g. 30 pence per Kg. excluding firing or 50 pence per Kg. to include firings.

14 Suppliers, Exhibitions and Bibliography

In this last chapter I intend to provide the hobby potter with a guide to a few books, exhibitions and suppliers that I consider may be of interest and assistance.

SUPPLIERS OF MATERIALS AND EQUIPMENT (UK)
Many pottery suppliers have very interesting and illustrative catalogues which they will send to you on application. These are worth studying and keeping for reference and will be sent to you free of charge. They will be necessary when ordering materials and equipment. In addition, some suppliers (e.g. Harrison Mayer Ltd.) issue monthly newsletters which they will send to you if you ask for your name to be put on their mailing list.

I list below some of the companies and their products that I recommend:

Podmore Ceramics Ltd,
103, Minet Road,
London SW9 7UH
Tel. 01-737 3636

Air hardening clay (Real clay)
All materials and equipment
Catalogue

Podmore & Sons Ltd,
Shelton,
Stoke-on-Trent,
Staffs.
Tel. 0782 24571

Air hardening clay (Real clay)
All materials and equipment
Catalogue

The Fulham Pottery Ltd,
Burlington House,
184, New Kings Road,
London SW6 4PB
Tel. 01-731 2167

Air hardening clay (Cold clay)
Materials and equipment
Catalouge

NB Air hardening clays are clays that can be left to dry in the air before cold glazing with a special non-toxic glaze which is applied with a brush. These clays are particularly suitable for model making.

Wengers Ltd, Garner Street, Etruria, Stoke-on-Trent ST4 7BQ Tel. 0782 25126	Materials and equipment Catalogue
Harrison Mayer Ltd, Craft and Education Division, Campbell Road, Stoke-on-Trent ST4 4ET Tel. 0782 414600	Materials and equipment Catalogue Newsletter
Potclays Ltd, Brick kiln Lane, Etruria, Stoke-on-Trent ST4 7BP Tel. 0782 29816	Materials and equipment Catalogue
Sneyd Ceramics, Sneyd Oxides Ltd, Sneyd Mills, Leonora Street, Stoke-on-Trent ST6 3BZ	Specialize in glazes for the once-firing of pottery
The Industrial Pyrometer Co. Ltd, (IPCO), 66-67, Gooch Street, North, Birmingham B5 6QY Tel. 021-622 3511	All forms of temperature indicators including pyrometers, midget non-indicating controllers and mini controllers which will switch off the kiln at a pre-set temperature.
Deancraft Ltd, Lovatt Street, Stoke-on-Trent, ST4 7RL Tel. 0782 411049	Materials and equipment Moulds a speciality Catalogue
Hymus Engineering Company, West Station Goods Yard, Maldon, Essex CM9 6SG Tel. 0621 52391	Competitively priced and highly recommended for kilns, pugmills and wheels. Personal after-sales service.

Acme Marls Ltd,   Kiln shelves and kiln furniture
Clough Street,
Hanley,
Stoke-on-Trent ST1 4AF
Tel. 0782 21541

Note: Most of the above companies have showrooms. If you should be in their vicinity it is worth taking the time to call in to see their products and discuss problems you have with them. They are all very helpful.

SUPPLIERS OF MATERIALS AND EQUIPMENT (USA)

American Art Clay Co,
4717 West 16th Street,
Indianapolis 24
Ind.

Cedar Heights Clay Company,
50 Portsmouth Road,
Oak Hill,
Ohio.

Craftools, Inc.
1 Industrial Road,
Wood-Ridge,
NJ 07076.

Gare Ceramic Supply Co,
165 Rosemont St,
Haverhill,
Mass.

Illinois Clay Products Co,
Barber Bldg,
Joliet,
Ill.

Langley Cermaic Studio,
413 South 24th St,
Philadelphia,
Pa.

Randall Wheel,
Box 774,
Alfred,
NY 14802.

Whittaker, Clarke and Daniels Inc.
260 West Broadway,
New York 13,
NY.

EXHIBITIONS OF POTTERY AND CERAMICS

These days there are usually many exhibitions of pottery and ceramics being held all around the country, ranging from large historical exhibitions in museums to the small local exhibition being held by a local craft potter. Do visit as many exhibitions as you can for they will help to increase your knowledge of the subject enormously and provide you with many new ideas to experiment with. Also there are usually people around who are only too willing to discuss and explain the pottery and ceramics in more detail.

For details of forthcoming exhibitions, look at a current issue of the Craftsmen Potters' Association magazine, *Ceramic Review*. There are always superb permanent exhibitions to be seen at:

a   The Craftsmen Potters' Shop,
William Blake House,
Marshall Street,
London W.1.

b   The Victoria and Albert Museum,
Exhibition Road,
London S.W.7.

c   The Fitzwilliam Museum,
Cambridge,

REFERENCE BOOKS

There are many pottery books on the market today, but some tend to be rather technical, which can be confusing for the beginner or hobby potter — hence one of my reasons for writing *this* book! However, there are several books that I feel would make useful additions to a collection — or even to borrow from a public library in order to read and make notes from.

I list some of these books below:

BALL and LOVOOS, *Making Pottery Without a Wheel*, Rheinhold
BATES, SHIRLEY, *Teaching Today: Pottery*, Batsford

SUPPLIERS, EXHIBITIONS AND BIBLIOGRAPHY

BILLINGTON, DORA M.. *The Technique of Pottery*, rev. John Colbeck
Batsford

CASSON, MICHAEL, *The Craft of the Potter*, BBC

COLBECK, JOHN, *Pottery, the Technique of Throwing*, Batsford

FOURNIER, ROBERT, *Illustrated Dictionary of Practical Pottery*, Van
Nostrand Reinhold

FRASER, H., *Kilns and Kiln Firing for the Craft Potter*, Pitman

LEACH, BERNARD, *A Potter's Book*, Faber and Faber

Ceramic Review: bi-monthly magazine issued by the Craftsmen Potters'
Association of Great Britain, 17a Newburgh Street, London W.1. (Tel.
01-439 3377)

Glossary

Agate: Pottery made from entwining coloured clays

Ash glaze: A glaze made from a wood ash and a clay, such as china clay. Different ashes create different colours and textures of glazes.

Ball clay: A plastic secondary clay which will fire to a high temperature.

Banding wheel: An unpowered turntable which can be used on a table for painting horizontal bands on to pottery or for supporting hand-built pots whilst being made.

Bat: A kiln shelf made from fireclay, or a wooden board for working on.

Bentonite: An ingredient added to glazes and slips as a suspender.

Biscuit: Unglazed pottery that has been fired once — usually to around 960° C (1760°F) for educational purposes.

Bloating: Blisters in the body of the pot usually occurr during glaze firing and caused by pressure exerted by gases which are trapped within the partially fused body.

Body: This is another word for the clay used to make pottery.

Burnishing: The technique of polishing leather-hard clay by rubbing it with the back of a spoon or a smooth stone.

Casting: To make pottery shapes by pouring liquid clay (slip) into a porous plaster of Paris mould.

Cone: A triangular shaped cone which has a known melting point and is placed inside a kiln to indicate the temperature reached at a given stage.

Crawling: When the fired glaze shrinks away from the body leaving bare patches. Often caused by dust or grease on the pottery before glazing.

Crazing: The appearance of fine cracking lines in the glaze caused by excessive contraction of the glaze during cooling. The pot then usually becomes porous as the glaze 'seal' is broken.

Cutting off: Pulling a thin wire or fishing line between pot and wheelhead before slicing it off.

Deflocculent: An electrolyte such as sodium silicate and soda ash which when added causes the clay slip or glaze to disperse and become more fluid.

Dottle: A sponge on the end of a stick used for cleaning and smoothing the inside of tall pots.

Dunting: When cold air gets into a kiln whilst it is cooling, causing the pots to crack or break.

Earthenware: A fairly porous pottery made from clay which is fired to a temperature below that at which it would vitrify — usually around 1060°C — 1080°C (1940°F — 1976°F) for educational purposes.

GLOSSARY

Enamels: Low-temperature coloured glazes — usually brightly coloured — that are applied, mostly by brush, on to a pre-fired high-temperature glaze.

Feathering: A technique of decoration using a feather or a bristle which is gently dragged across lines of wet coloured slip.

Fettling: The removal of seams and marks caused usually by casting moulds. The leather-hard clay is scraped with a knife or metal kidney or sponged.

Firing: The heating up of a kiln packed with pottery to a temperature that will make the clay and/or the glaze hard and permanent.

Fuse: To heat to melting point.

Glaze: A thin layer of glass covering a biscuit-fired pot. Usually the biscuit-fired pot is dipped, brushed or sprayed with a suspension of ground glaze in water and then fired to a high temperature.

Glost: The actual firing of glazed ware in a kiln.

Greenware: Unfired clayware.

Grog: A sand-like material made from ground-up biscuit ware which is added to clay to give it strength and reduce shrinkage.

Hand-building: The term used for building pottery or making pots in any way other than by using a potter's wheel or mechanical means. It usually refers to methods such as slab building, coiling or pinching.

Incising: A form of decoration — marking and incising the surface of leather-hard clay with tools.

Kidney: A kidney-shaped flat rubber or metal tool, useful for smoothing and finishing hand-built pottery and pots made on a wheel.

Kiln: An oven for firing pottery to a very high temperature. A kiln can be fuelled by electricity, gas, oil or solid fuels.

Kiln furniture: A term used to describe the refractory pieces used in a kiln to support and separate the shelves and pieces of pottery during firing.

Knuckling up: The action of raising a pot on a wheel by gently squeezing the wall of the pot between the knuckle of the first finger of the right hand and the middle finger of the left hand.

Lawn: A fine-mesh sieve supported by a frame and used in pottery for passing liquid slips and glazes through.

Leather-hard: A term used for clay that has partly dried to a stage when it can be cut like leather, using a knife. At this stage the clay is still damp enough to join handles, knobs etc., with slip, to a pot in the same condition. It is the ideal state for turning, fettling and sponging. Another name for this stage is 'cheese-hard'.

Maturing temperature: This is the term to describe the temperature reached when a glaze will have properly fused or when clay has been fired to its correct strength.

Opening up: Inserting the thumb of the right hand into the centred ball of clay and drawing it outwards.

Once-fired: A term used when pottery is made, glazed and fired in one operation — sometimes called 'clay glazing' or 'raw glazing'.

On-glaze: A form of decoration whereby metal oxides and stains are applied on top of the unfired glaze.

Overfiring: When pottery has reached a temperature in the kiln in excess of its optimum temperature. The pottery is often distorted and, if glazed the pots frequently stick to the kiln shelves.

Oxides: Metal-based clay or glaze colorants.

Pinholing: Usually a fault in the glaze or clay body causing tiny bubbles of trapped air to break through the glaze or body at high temperature.

Plasticity: The quality that clay has when it can be shaped easily and yet retain its new shape.

Porcelain: White translucent stoneware clay, firing to temperatures in excess of $1300°C$ ($2372°C$).

Porous: The porous state of biscuit ware will indicate the thickness of the glaze to be used. It relates to the amount of pore space in the ware.

Primary: A primary clay is a pure clay.

Props: Supports that separate kiln shelves.

Pulling: Pulling handles is the action of stroking plastic clay downwards with water, using the hands.

Pugging: The action of reconstituting clay by passing it through a pug mill, which is a form of mincing machine.

Pyrometer: A clock-type temperature indicator sited near a kiln and attached to a thermocouple which is inserted into the kiln in order to record the internal temperature of the kiln.

Raku: A thick type of low-fired earthenware, used in Japan for the traditional tea ceremony. The pots are removed from the kiln, whilst it is still firing, with tongs, and then plunged into water. Sometimes they are first plunged into leaves or sawdust to produce varying colour effects.

Refractory clays: Those clays capable of withstanding high temperatures, in excess of $1300°C$ ($2372°F$). Stoneware and porcelain clays are examples of these.

Rolling guides: Sticks of wood approximately 35 cm. (14 in.) long x 5 mm. (¼ in.) thick used in conjunction with a rolling pin to produce rolled clay of even thickness.

Secondary clays: These are clays that contain a variety of minerals and are, consequently, not pure.

Sgraffito: A form a decoration whereby an outer coating of clay or glaze is scratched through with a sharp tool to expose the different colour beneath.

Slip: A liquid clay with the consistency of double cream, used in conjunction with colouring oxides for decoration. Also used for slip moulding.

Slip trailing: A decorative process for creating designs by forcing liquid clay through a narrow nozzle attached to a bag or bottle, like icing a cake.

Slurry: An alternative name for slip.

Soak: To hold the temperature of a kiln steady for about 20 minutes. This will improve the quality of certain glazes.

Sponging: Cleaning the surface of clayware prior to firing, using a damp sponge.

GLOSSARY

Sprigging: A form of decoration by fixing small moulded shapes to the surface of a pot of a different colour — e.g. Wedgwood.

Stains: Colours prepared from oxides for staining clays and glazes.

Stoneware: Pottery fired to a temperature above $1200°C$ ($2192°F$) which is vitreous (non-porous) and opaque.

Texturing: A decorative process applied to clay whilst it is still soft, causing a roughened or indented surface.

Throwing: The making of a pot with the hands, a potter's wheel and plastic clay.

Turning: Trimming thrown pots at the leather-hard stage to remove excess clay, using a potter's wheel and sharp metal tools.

Underglaze: Oxides and stains applied to greenware prior to biscuit firing and then glazed.

Vitrify: To fire to a glassy state which is non-porous.

Wax resist: A wax applied to a biscuit-fired pot so that it will resist glaze. Usually applied to parts of a pot as a decorative process.

Weathering: Leaving clay outside exposed to the weather.

Wedging: The process of de-airing clay by hand. The lump of clay is repeatedly cut and thrown down hard on to a solid work bench.

Wheel: A revolving turntable controlled by the potter's feet or by electricity. It can revolve at varying speeds according to the potter's requirements.

Temperature table

Centigrade°	Fahrenheit°
200	392
400	752
600	1112
730	1346
760	1400
800	1472
900	1652
960	1760
980	1796
1000	1832
1050	1922
1060	1940
1080	1976
1100	2012
1150	2102
1200	2192
1250	2282
1260	2300
1280	2336
1300	2372
1400	2552

Index

INDEX